W9-BAC-945

Also by Ibtisam Barakat

TASTING THE SKY:
A Palestinian Childhood

IBTISAM BARAKAT

BALCONY ON THE MOON

The author at age seventeen

IBTISAM BARAKAT

BALCONY ON THE MOON

COMING OF AGE IN PALESTINE

Margaret Ferguson Books

Farrar Straus Giroux

New York

RELEASED FROM

SOUTH PASADENA PUBLIC LIBRARY
1100 OXLEY STREET
SOUTH PASADENA, CA 91030

Farrar Straus Giroux Books for Young Readers
An imprint of Macmillan Publishing Group, LLC
175 Fifth Avenue, New York 10010

Copyright © 2016 by Ibtisam Barakat
All rights reserved
Map designed by Cathy Bobak
Compass rose designed by Freepik
Printed in the United States of America
First edition, 2016
1   3   5   7   9   10   8   6   4   2

fiercereads.com

Library of Congress Cataloging-in-Publication Data

Names: Barakat, Ibtisam, author.
Title: Balcony on the moon : coming of age in Palestine / Ibtisam Barakat.
Description: First edition. | New York : Farrar Straus Giroux Books for Young
    Readers, 2016. | "Margaret Ferguson Books"—Title page.
Identifiers: LCCN 2015039502 (print) | LCCN 2016006614 (ebook) |
    ISBN 9780374302511 (hardback) | ISBN 9780374302535 (Ebook)
Subjects: LCSH: Barakat, Ibtisam—Childhood and youth. | Children,
    Palestinian Arab—Biography—Juvenile literature. | Youth, Palestinian
    Arab—Biography—Juvenile literature. | Girls—Education—Arab
    countries—Juvenile literature. | Arab-Israeli conflict—Juvenile
    literature. | BISAC : JUVENILE NONFICTION / Biography & Autobiography /
    Political. | JUVENILE NONFICTION / Biography & Autobiography / Cultural
    Heritage. | JUVENILE NONFICTION / Family / Multigenerational.
Classification: LCC DS119.7 .B28445 2016 (print) | LCC DS119.7 (ebook) | DDC
    956.95/2044092—dc23
LC record available at http://lccn.loc.gov/2015039502

Our books may be purchased in bulk for promotional, educational, or business use.
Please contact your local bookseller or the Macmillan Corporate and Premium Sales
Department at (800) 221-7945 ext. 5442 or by e-mail at
MacmillanSpecialMarkets@macmillan.com.

An earlier version of the chapter "Stone House" was published as
"Radio Street" by *The Massachusetts Review* in 2014.
Some names have been changed in the story to honor
the preferences of individuals.

To Arabic and English, the two languages of my pen.
Arabic moves on the page from right to left. English
moves from left to right. They meet in my heart,
forming a bridge of peace between East and West.

To my family members, the Barakats.

To my people, the Palestinians.

To our Qur'anic and Biblical cousins, the Jews.

To everyone who helps create more kindness
among the peoples of the world and more healing
for the family of humanity.

And to readers everywhere.

CONTENTS

AUTHOR'S NOTE

When I mention that I am Palestinian, I am often asked: But where is Palestine on the map? Palestine is a geographic region in the Middle East that has come under the military control of many nations throughout history. In the twentieth century, Palestine was ruled by the Ottoman Empire until World War I. Britain followed with a military mandate over Palestine that lasted until 1948.

Because of the Holocaust and extensive Jewish immigration to Palestine with the aim of making it a national home for Jews, the region experienced enormous violence between various groups. Britain promised to facilitate a homeland for Jews and suppressed Palestinian aspirations for freedom. The newly formed United Nations then partitioned Palestine in a manner that resulted in a war between Jews and Arabs in 1948. At the end of that war, Israel was established on three quarters of the land that had been owned by Palestinians, and most of the Palestinians became displaced, a loss the Palestinians call the *Nakba*, the Catastrophe. In its General Assembly Resolution 194, the United Nations aimed to facilitate a peaceful return of the Palestinian refugees to their homes. However, the resolution was not implemented.

Jordan and Egypt governed the remaining quarter of Palestine until 1967, when the Six-Day War occurred, ending with Israel occupying the West Bank and East Jerusalem, the Gaza Strip, and other areas. Palestinians call this outcome the *Naksa*, the Setback. All of historic Palestine was then replaced by Israel on the world map. In its Security Council Resolution 242, the UN attempted to solve the conflict of Palestine and Israel by proposing a two-state solution. However, this resolution also was not implemented. Consequently, the prolonged absence of a satisfactory solution continues to generate violence.

Recognizing that many countries helped to alleviate the homelessness of the Jews as a people by making a home for them in Palestine, and that this resulted in the Palestinians becoming a homeless people, the United Nations formed the United Nations Relief and Works Agency for Palestine Refugees in the Near East, UNRWA. It is the largest UN agency dedicated to providing refugees of one displaced people with basic protection, housing, education, and health services.

Without the help of the UNRWA, which offered education to generations of Palestinian refugees, including me, *Balcony on the Moon* would not have been written.

Believing that childhood and coming-of-age stories unite the world, I hope that *Balcony on the Moon* will encourage many young people—and adults, too—to share their experiences toward the composition of an ongoing book of life that represents all of humanity and ensures inclusion, safety, dignity, and freedom for all people now and for future generations.

We once lived rooted
Like the ancient olive trees.
Now we're birds
Nesting on songs
About homes we miss.
Storms and distances
Decide our address.
—Ibtisam Barakat

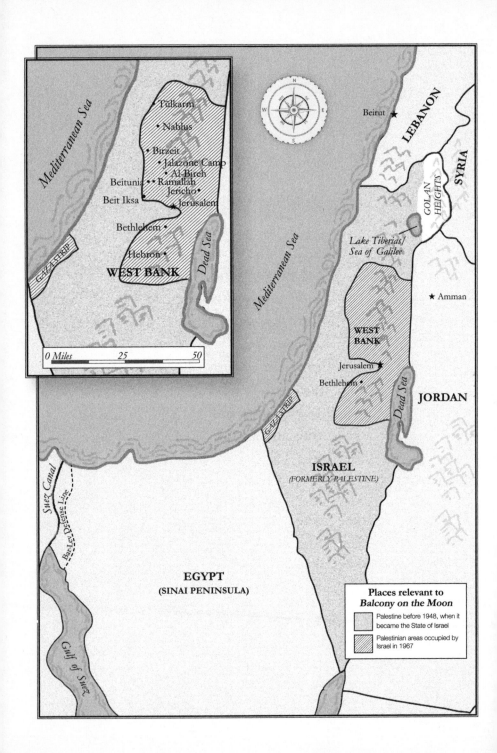

Tulkarm

Nablus

Birzeit

Jalazone Camp

Al-Bireh

Beitunia

Ramallah

Jericho

Beit Iksa

Jerusalem

Bethlehem

Hebron

WEST BANK

Mediterranean Sea

GAZA STRIP

Dead Sea

0 Miles   25   50

N
NW   NE
W   E
SW   SE
S

Beirut ★

LEBANON

SYRIA

GOLAN HEIGHTS

Lake Tiberias/
Sea of Galilee

Mediterranean Sea

★ Amman

**WEST
BANK**

Jerusalem ★

Bethlehem •

JORDAN

Dead Sea

ISRAEL
(FORMERLY PALESTINE)

GAZA STRIP

Suez Canal

Bar-Lev Defense Line

EGYPT
(SINAI PENINSULA)

Gulf of Suez

Places relevant to
Balcony on the Moon

Palestine before 1948, when it
became the State of Israel

Palestinian areas occupied by
Israel in 1967

PART I

Radio Street
1971–1973

Stone House

Grandmother Fatima has just arrived at our new apartment on Radio Street, on the northern side of Ramallah in the West Bank. She is carrying her woven bamboo basket filled with green almonds from her village in Jerusalem. She does not say whether she likes or dislikes our new place. When I ask her she says, "All that matters is that we are in the same country and I can visit you." She then asks me to remind her how old I am, what school I go to now, and what grade I am in. I tell Grandma that I am seven and a half years old, still go to the Jalazone Girls' School, run by the United Nations Relief and Works Agency (UNRWA), and will soon complete the second grade. I am about to show her that I can write my name and many other words, but I stop when I remember that she has never gone to school and cannot read or write.

Mother and Grandma go to the kitchen. I follow them

quietly, hoping to listen in on their conversation and learn about the strange world of grownups and its many surprises—marriages, money, deaths, and whispered problems about relationships.

Today Grandma is speaking about Aunt Amina, one of Mother's two sisters. Aunt Amina lives in Amman, Jordan. She has ten daughters and no sons, and her husband, Nimer, insists he wants a boy to carry on his name. Nimer is a professor at a university, and everyone in our family calls him *mitaallem,* educated.

Grandma is worried about Aunt Amina's safety because seven months ago, in the middle of September 1970, thousands of Palestinians living in Jordan were killed when the fedayeen, the Palestinian freedom fighters, and the Jordanian army had one of their worst battles. The hostilities began even before September and haven't ended yet.

The fedayeen wanted to gain more political and military control inside Jordan in order to fight Israel from the Jordanian border so they could take back Palestine from Israel and return to the homes and cities they lost first in the war of 1948, which displaced the majority of Palestinians, and then in the Six-Day War, which ended with Israel controlling all Palestinian lands.

The fedayeen hoped that Jordan would help them in their fight against Israel. But the Jordanian leaders did not want the fedayeen to organize non-Jordanian military groups inside their country. So the two sides fought, and the Jordanian army won after a massacre of Palestinians so grim that the month of Ayloul is now called Ayloul al-Aswad, Black September. Those words make me think of a whole month without the sun rising once.

"Every time I pray, I leave on the prayer rug big questions that I believe only Allah can answer," Grandma says. "They are about the future and what will happen in this woeful Holy Land. But even after I pray, the questions are still there in my mind and in the world." She raises her arms to the sky pleading: *"La-aimta ya rab?"* Dear God, until when?

"Nothing in our lives is predictable, but let's not despair," Mother says.

Mother and Grandma begin to exchange happier family stories, entangled with names, nicknames, and half events. They finish each other's sentences, and I try to understand and arrange in my mind the names of my relatives, especially those whom I have not met because they live in other countries, or those who have died but continue to live in these stories as I learn new pieces of how they fit into our family history.

When Grandma gets up to leave, I take her basket and walk with her to the bus stop near the giant radio tower with the frightening skull-shaped high-voltage danger signs that order people to stay away. Radio Street is named after this broadcast tower, which was built by the British forces when they ruled over Palestine after World War I. Perhaps from this day on, every time Grandma Fatima listens to a radio program, she will think of us.

When the bus leaves, carrying Grandma with it, I try to guess how she feels about our new apartment. I hope she dislikes it, because ever since we moved here, one month ago, I have been trying to convince myself to like it, but in my heart I do not.

Most of me still lives at the stone house we left behind on top of a hill near Nablus Road on the northeastern side of Ramallah. There, I often hid behind big rocks or lay on them, feeling their warm backs against my own. I picked colorful wildflowers and crushed them to use as finger paint on the rocks. I played with turtles on the gravel road, removing obstacles from their paths, sometimes carrying them and running so they would reach their homes faster. I also liked to place bread crumbs on their backs for them to take to their children.

I think about that house every day, but it is no longer made of stone. Now it is made of memories—hours spent watching migrating birds in the sky, waiting for dinner, for Mother to come home after shopping trips, or for Father to come home from driving his truck.

I remember the toys my older brothers created: cars they built from thin, colorful electrical wires; skateboards constructed from wooden vegetable boxes fixed on ball bearings they got from abandoned car tires; kites made with bamboo stalks and newspaper glued together with bread dough; musical instruments shaped from rubber bands strung over a cooking pan; slingshots carved from tree branches; and origami rockets tied to strings and then to Mother's clothesline and left to fly all day.

I can also change my memories as I choose. The garden in front of the house now has magical plants that grow both fruits and vegetables. Rain never falls, except right into designated water containers or within the borders of the front garden. Sometimes a passing purple cloud rains sweet black grapes. We all open our mouths to catch and eat them.

My parents bought the stone house five years ago, when I was two and a half years old, right after the birth of my sister, Mona. And even though only my youngest brother, Samer, was born there, a year ago, and the rest of us children were born in various cities—Basel, who's ten and a half, and I in Jerusalem; Muhammad, who's nine and a half, in Jericho; and Mona, who's five, in al-Bireh—I feel as though all of us were born there.

We left the stone house once before, four years ago, on June 5, 1967, when the Six-Day War started. We had to run from shelter to shelter and from fear to fear as Israeli, Egyptian, Syrian, and Jordanian armies fought. The six days became one hundred and thirty-five days for us because it took that long before we could return to Ramallah with the help of the United Nations and the International Red Cross. At the end of the war, Ramallah was occupied by Israel and we began to live as refugees in our own homes and on our own land, with no right to travel to other countries and be assured that we could come back, no right to cultivate most of the lands we owned, and no right to build new homes or start new businesses without the permission of *al-hakem al-askari*, the Israeli military ruler. But when we returned and lived in the stone house again, that helped me to remember how I had felt before the war: happy and safe.

Then Israeli soldiers started to come daily to train on our hillside. We could see them outside our window as they set up camps surrounded by barbed wire. They ran drills and practiced shooting at cardboard cutouts shaped like people, leaving those targets with countless bullet holes that bled air.

My siblings and I found many ways to become less afraid of the soldiers, including climbing the barbed wire around their camps after they left for the day, playing hide-and-seek inside the trenches they had dug, gathering empty bullet shells, and peeking through the holes in the cardboard people—it was like looking through binoculars into a smaller world.

But then some soldiers began to knock on the door when Father was at work. They asked for a drink of water, even though they carried water bottles. They looked at Mother as though she was the water they wanted to drink. Each time, Mother pointed from the window to our well, which the soldiers could use to refill their bottles; then we pulled the curtains shut, made certain that our door was locked, and pushed all the furniture we could gather against it. We watched the soldiers from the slits between the curtains.

We could no longer go outside, except after the army left for the evening. So my parents decided to leave the stone house forever. They sold it and searched for a different place for us to move to. We came here. I wish we hadn't, and that the Israeli soldiers had gone to train somewhere else instead.

This new house is a one-story white stone villa that looks like a giant ship sailing on a green grass sea. There is a small orchard and a hedge that surrounds everything like the edges of a huge box.

Our apartment is in the basement, so that we can be hidden from all eyes like rabbits in a burrow. Mother especially is happier underground, in this war-shelter-like place. But Father, although he says nothing about the move, appears sad. He was proud to own the house we lived in, proud of improving it as he liked. Here he cannot change anything, and there is no space for him to keep a goat and sing to it every evening like he did in the stone house. Singing helps Father feel happier.

Basel and Muhammad are content to run and play in a nearby meadow with other boys who gather for soccer games. But I continue to be afraid because the news on the radio speaks daily about death and fighting in many places. I do not know how far away the places they mention are from our house.

Father tries to help me overcome some of my anxious feelings. He explains that Vietnam is not nearby and the war there is not about us. Because Grandma's village in Jerusalem is called Beit Iksa—and dozens of other Palestinian villages begin with *Beit*—and because *nam* is also a word in Arabic, I had thought Vietnam was Beit Nam, and that its war was also near us.

Only when I enter the imaginative world of a story do I win

against the fear of war beginning again and destroying every-thing. Stories take me on an adventure and change my feelings, as though I am not me, but the main character in the story. I love becoming Sinbad, the fictional Arabian sailor. As I sail into mysteries, monsters hide everywhere, but I battle them and triumph, and always return home, bringing back gifts for everyone who waits for me.

I also triumph over fear by listening to old people tell of memories that bring peaceful, faraway worlds to me. I like how their faces light up when they describe the happy times of *hur-reyyah*, freedom. Their words give me hope and chase away my fears.

Baba Noel

Our apartment consists of an L-shaped space that has two main rooms, one big and one small. The small room has a large window that brings in fresh orchard breezes. This room is where my siblings and I spread a straw rug on the floor, place our mattresses on top of it, and sleep at night. In the morning we stack the mattresses neatly and roll up the rug so the room can be used for daytime activities.

The big room has a long, horizontal glass panel up high that lets in light. But unlike the window, the panel cannot be opened. So the first day of our move, Mother stood on a chair, then on her toes, stretching herself all the way to reach the glass, and with red lipstick drew a big sun on it. "This way it will always be sunny," she said, smiling as she jumped back to the floor.

Between the two rooms is a tiny kitchen that has a gas stove instead of the small and dangerous three-legged *baboor* that sat in a corner of the stone house. Mother had to fill the *baboor* with kerosene over and over and warned us repeatedly to stay away from it. But children playing in the house, especially our young relatives when visiting, sometimes knocked off a boiling pot of food. My right leg has a scar from a burn from that *baboor.*

For the first time, we have hot and cold running water. This makes Mother dance as she turns the faucet on and off. Dancing is the way she celebrates. She announces that she does not ever again want to live anywhere without running water.

We also have a shower. After my sister, Mona, tried it for the first time and shouted for help when the hot water suddenly turned cold, I explained that a shower is like a private cloud. It will rain when we want it to. But because the heating of this cloud is done by solar panels, the temperature of the shower is up to the sun and weather, not us. Whenever someone uses the shower, Mona runs to announce that they are inside the cloud.

The biggest new addition to our life, however, is electric light. In each room a bulb hangs at the end of a long wire that dangles from the ceiling. When I want to turn the light on, I move the switch extremely slowly to savor the thrilling moment when the bulb comes to life and glows like a pear-shaped private moon. When the bulb swings from an evening breeze, big and small shadows dance across our walls. Mother holds up the hem of her dress and dances with them.

Because electricity is expensive, Father makes certain we do not waste any of it. He says every minute of light costs him a minute of work. So when I want to stay up and read at night,

Father and I agree that I can have half an hour of light if I am willing to tell him some stories from the books I read. This way he can continue his education. Father completed only one and a half grades of school because when he was a child Britain imposed heavy fees on Palestinian schools, leaving many parents forced to choose either food and clothing or education for their children. Jealous of the boys whose families could afford school fees, and sad that he had to work at a rock quarry at age eight, Father taught himself whenever he could and memorized parts of the Qur'an, the holy book of Islam, and many poems. But he does not read well enough to start a book and finish it.

However, he does know stories that have been told to him—religious and historical, and many parts of a long folktale called "Taghreebat Bani Hilal" (The diaspora of the Banu Hilal tribe). Their name means descendants of the crescent moon. In this half-real, half-fictitious story, Father says the main characters remain the same, but the story varies from city to city and country to country depending on the storyteller, so the plot is always full of surprises and you can hear it many times without knowing it completely.

Within the first month after we move into our apartment, Mother follows the Palestinian custom of introducing our family to our new neighbors by sending me to deliver a plate of delicious food to each of them.

"You are the *safeerah*, our ambassador," she explains. "This is an important responsibility. The neighbors will judge all of us by how you behave when they meet you. Do not pester them with questions; just deliver the food." She shakes her hands up and down for emphasis, and waits for me to nod that I understand. "Remember to greet the person who opens the door by saying, '*Marhabah*, hello, I am the daughter of your new neighbor, Um Basel, Mother of Basel. Please accept this food from her.' Any questions?"

"Yes," I reply, even though I know the question I have is one she doesn't want to hear. "Why do you always have to be called Um Basel? Can't you be called Mother of Ibtisam on some days?" I ask for the hundredth time, although she has explained that a mother in Arab culture is called by the name of her first male child. "Can't we change that custom in our family?"

As usual, she ignores me, and that makes me sad every time because I do not ever count in her name, not even on my birthday.

As Mother's ambassador, I first go to meet the old man who lives above our apartment and owns the entire building. His name is Haj Hamd Allah. He always wears white-and-sky-blue-striped pajamas and a white knit cap, and carries the traditional phosphorous glow-in-the-dark *masbahah* of thirty-three prayer beads. Both Father and Grandma Fatima have a *masbahah*. It means that a person praises and thanks Allah all the time.

Haj Hamd Allah's apartment is on top of our half of the basement and has a glass-enclosed veranda. He sits there in the afternoons to rest. We can see him from the street. When he goes inside, we hear his footsteps moving above us like a slow bear, and we know exactly which room he is in.

Haj Hamd Allah watches me suspiciously as I climb the white stone steps that lead to his veranda, then stand at the door holding the plate of food. He seems to dislike children as much as I dislike his frown.

He calls for his granddaughter, Izdehar, to answer, and I am relieved. I met Izdehar shortly after we moved in. She visits him at the end of every week to cook his food, wash his clothes, and clean his house. For her last chore, Izdehar rolls up her sleeves to her elbows, her pants to her knees, and stands on a chair to clean the glass of the veranda. Then, with soapy water thick with bubbles, she scrubs the white stone steps.

The second time Izdehar and I spoke, she asked me if her grandfather goes out during the day. I told her that he only goes out occasionally to harvest some fruit from the trees in his orchard. Even though I did not mention that his frown frightens me, she said that Haj Hamd Allah is a kind man but has become withdrawn since her grandmother died.

Now Izdehar takes the plate and nudges her grandfather, who says to me, "I told your parents that you must stay away from my fruit trees, including the ones near your door. But I've changed my mind. Choose an apple and a plum tree to harvest."

I thank him and fly down the steps to tell Mother the news; then in minutes I am back at his door: "Mother says we will prune the orchard in return." As Haj Hamd Allah shows a rare smile, he also shows his perfect white set of dentures. When I leave I am glad that he is happy. But the pruning, I think, will not only help him, it may help console Father for the loss of his goat because Father also loves to garden.

The second visit I make is to Um Ibrahim, the woman who lives in the other half of the basement. She wears a colorfully embroidered black *thawb*, the traditional Palestinian dress for women, and a white shawl, and has one brown eye and one blue eye. Seeing the food, she praises Mother's thoughtfulness and wants to know more about our family, especially the number of children.

"Three boys and two girls," I say. "The oldest is ten and a half, and the youngest is one."

"*Ma sha' Allah*, children are blessings," she replies.

"My parents want to have two more boys, so we will be five boys and two girls when that happens."

Um Ibrahim laughs. "But what if the babies are girls?"

"My parents prayed for boys only, and I am certain that Allah listens to people's prayers."

Against Mother's instructions not to do anything but deliver the food, I ask Um Ibrahim about herself.

"Come," she says. "I will show you." She leads me to a room that has two giant shiny steel containers. Together they are the size of a big bed and fill up most of the space. When she opens the first container, waves and waves of steam rise up as though the contents are boiling. But when I look inside I realize that the containers hold tubs of red and yellow ice cream.

"I make ice cream and my son Ibrahim transports it in thermoses to sell in villages every day. That is how we earn a living."

I stand there mesmerized with pleasure, breathing in the fragrance of vanilla. I open my mouth to lick the ice cream fog and chase it with my tongue. Um Ibrahim laughs.

I have heard Ibrahim's motorcycle's annoying loud noise and seen the thermoses secured behind him, but never guessed that only a wall separated me and my family from a roomful of ice cream. Um Ibrahim empties the plate I brought to her, washes it, and fills it with the two flavors: strawberry and vanilla. She gives me sugar cones, too. The surprise at home turns our day into a feast. We do not have a refrigerator, so we eat it all at once.

The last family that lives in our building is the Asfoors. Their apartment is identical to Haj Hamd Allah's, including a glass-enclosed veranda. But while Haj Hamd Allah's veranda has a prayer rug showing the ninety-nine names of Allah, the Asfoors' veranda has a big painting of the Virgin Mary holding baby Jesus.

Mr. and Mrs. Asfoor stay home like Haj Hamd Allah. They have a son and a daughter, Nicholas and Camellia, in their twenties, and a young son, Issa, who is my age. Nicholas and Camellia go to work every weekday, but Nicholas works full-time and Camellia works half a day, coming home early to help her mother with housework.

It is Camellia who answers my knock. After taking the food, she offers me a cup of lemonade, which I drink. Gazing at the large painting of the Virgin Mary, I want to ask Camellia about

Christianity but wonder if Mother would be upset if she knew. I ask anyway.

I tell her that although my family is Muslim, one of Grandma's sisters became a Christian nun. That happened during the Great Depression, when many Western countries faced extreme economic hardships. Palestine and other regions that had come under British control after World War I, and had their political and economic lives ruled by Britain, faced severe hardships, too. A church adopted Grandma's sister and changed her name from Amenah to Mary. Now she lives in a convent in the Old City of Jerusalem, near the Church of the Holy Sepulchre. Because Mother calls her Aunt Mary, all of us do, too.

As a nun, Aunt Mary cannot marry or have children. She spends her days reading the Bible, praying, lighting candles, working for the church, and studying history, using the several languages she knows. She rarely speaks about Christianity to us. The only time she did was when she mentioned the name of Allah in a conversation. I asked her if Christians believe in Allah like Muslims do. She explained that as an Arab Christian she prays to Allah using the same name for God that Muslims use. *Allah* is the Arabic word that describes the One God that Abraham, Moses, Jesus, and Muhammad believed in. The Hebrew Bible has the word *Elohim*.

Camellia acts like Aunt Mary. She does not want to talk about Christianity but says that she likes being a Christian living in Ramallah. She feels it is sacred to walk on the same land where Yasūaa', Jesus, walked and grew up.

"His footsteps are right here, under our footsteps," she says. "His voice is under our voices."

"What did Jesus say?" I ask.

"Love your neighbor!" she replies, smiling.

That makes me feel wonderful. Camellia is telling me that it is important to be good to your neighbors. I know that Islam says this, too. I wish someone could tell me how many religions there are in the world and what they believe.

Camellia then fills the plate I brought with a food I have never eaten before: living snails, inside their shells. "Take them to your mother," she says. "Tell her they are delicious sautéed in garlic and olive oil."

I take the snails to Mother and she asks that I deposit them, one by one, inside the stone wall around the orchard so that they can go on living.

"Are they a Christian food?" I ask. Muslims, unlike Christians, don't eat pork or drink alcohol. Maybe we aren't allowed to eat snails either.

"I only cook what your father can eat, and snails are not among your father's foods," she says.

In December, the Asfoor family sets up a tree decorated with lights in their glass veranda. It changes the feeling of the entire street. They are preparing to observe Christmas. I have not seen Christmas lights so close before. After looking at their tree, I make a finger-size one from pencil shavings that I glue around a stick planted inside a cup of dried mud. Small dots from Mother's red nail polish are the lights. As I hear Christmas hymns played on the radio, I admire my tree.

Issa tells me that Baba Noel, Santa Claus, will be coming in the middle of the night on Christmas Eve to give him a present.

"In the middle of the night? Is he not afraid?" I ask.

"Santa only works at night. He is not a normal person."

Camellia adds that Baba Noel travels the world on a sleigh pulled by deer to help celebrate the birth of Jesus, which happened centuries ago in the city of Bethlehem, less than an hour from where we live in Ramallah.

"Is Santa's sleigh similar to Aladdin's magic carpet?" I ask.

"He has reindeer helping. Aladdin has a genie," Issa says.

On Christmas Eve I find every excuse possible to open the door and run outside to see if Baba Noel has arrived in our neighborhood. I want to glimpse him even if for a second. Finally, Mother locks the door and puts the key in her pocket. I stand by the window waiting, but in spite of myself, I fall asleep before midnight.

I wake up to my parents speaking. "Who could be knocking at this hour?" Father says.

"I hope they are not soldiers," Mother murmurs. My brothers and sister quickly wake up, too.

Standing near but not opening the door, Father asks, *"Meen elly barra?"* Who is outside?

The answer comes back gently, almost like a whisper, accompanied by a tiny bell ringing softly: "Baba Noel."

"Baba who?" Father has no idea who Santa Claus is.

The voice answers again: "Baba Noel looking for Issa."

Now Father opens the door to see Santa's face, beard, and red suit.

I shout that Issa's apartment is on the other side of the building.

Soon after, my parents, brothers, sister, and I hear a car drive off.

"He is only a man wearing a costume," Mother explains, hoping to calm us down. "I can make a suit like his and let you wear it, too. Now go to sleep!"

But I stay up thinking about Issa's present. The next day when he does not volunteer to tell me what Santa gave him, I do not ask. But I ask everyone in my family what they would want if Santa could bring them something.

Muhammad: The best food, and to be the strongest person in the world so no one can hit me...

Mona: A whole shop of beautiful clothes and toys...

Mother: To become rich and spend all my time learning new things...

Basel: No one has asked me this before. I want to think about it longer before answering...

Me: One big book that has all the stories of the world in it, and a tree that grows pens and pencils...

Father: Freedom, and a cure for narcolepsy...

Everyone nods their heads, adding to their wishes a cure for narcolepsy.

Fingerprints

It is the middle of February, the month nicknamed *shbat al-khabbat*, the batterer, because of the big cold storms that whip our world. Outside, the wind is whistling. A thick fog is making it hard to see the orchard from our window. It has not stopped raining all day. There is so much rain that the large well in the yard filled up as fast as if it were a teacup. I am happy that February is a short month.

We are gathered around the tall green space heater, rubbing our hands together for warmth as we wait for Father to come home from work. The chattering of our teeth magnifies the trembling of our hearts.

"*Ta'akhkhar ktheer!* He is so late," Mother says. She bites her lip and holds back tears. She also holds her pregnant belly. There is nothing she can do. Father does not tell us where he goes each day because he does not know his destination. After he leaves in the morning, he drives to places he is told to go to pick up or deliver goods, and comes home in the evening not wanting to speak of work, except on the days when he reaches the sea or visits a new city, town, or village. He also tells us about when he passes by old Palestinian towns that have become depopulated because of wars and are now nothing but names and neglected ruins. He has seen many of them when they were full of people, so he describes to us how they were in the past, too, and with his words he brings them back to life for us.

My brothers Basel and Muhammad are passing the anxious time by talking about the accident our father had in Jerusalem several months ago during a school vacation when they were with him. Because Father has narcolepsy, he often falls asleep while driving, so Basel and Muhammad, when not in school, accompany him so they can wake him up if he falls asleep. Whenever his head droops, they shout and shake him. He usually wakes up quickly. But the accident last year left Father with broken ribs and Basel with his arm in a cast for weeks.

Father's narcolepsy has worsened over time. It started when he was twenty-five years old, ten years before he married Mother, and he has tried many medicines and ways to cope. But even the three electric-shock treatments he received from doctors in Jordan could not heal him.

He falls asleep while doing anything. It can happen every five minutes or every few hours. Sometimes, halfway through dinner, his spoon hangs in the air, then drops from his hand. As he sleeps, Father slides lower and lower in his seat.

When guests visit us, he often closes his eyes while they speak to him. After he wakes up, he is confused and embarrassed. But everyone ignores what has happened, and someone makes a quick summary of what has been said so he can rejoin the conversation.

Father takes many anti-sleeping pills, prescribed for him by a psychiatrist in East Jerusalem, drinks mud-thick coffee and deep-dark tea, but all of this has become ineffective. I am disappointed in medicine for not offering a cure for narcolepsy and wish the famous Muslim doctor Ibn Sīnā could come from the eleventh century to the twentieth and help him.

Father fights for his life every work hour as he tries to stay awake while driving, especially because the hum of the road lulls him to sleep behind the wheel. In Islam we believe in angels, so I imagine that Allah sends many angels who work frantically to make sure that Father is safe.

We have begged him to find different work, but driving is the only job Father loves to do. He makes clear to all of us that he will continue getting up at dawn, before the sun rises, praying to Allah, then going to work, until he is dead. "Have your feelings and let me work." He shrugs. "What other family in the world has a father who can drive with his eyes closed?"

Finally we hear heavy steps splashing in the puddles outside and see Father appear in the fog. He is swaying left and right, and we see that he is holding his hand tightly.

"Take me to the hospital," he mutters the moment Mother opens the door.

There is blood on his wet clothes.

Instantly I am at the Asfoors', knocking on their door and explaining that Father is hurt and asking them to make a phone call for a taxi to take him to the hospital.

When the taxi arrives, Father, leaning on Nicholas and supported by my older brothers and the driver, is driven to the hospital. I write a prayer in the form of a letter to Allah asking for forgiveness for any mistakes I might have made that contributed to Allah making Father get hurt, and then I ask Allah to protect Father's life.

Father comes home early the next morning with a bandaged hand and a pale complexion. Several days later he is able to speak about the accident for the first time.

He says that even though he lost part of his thumb, he is happy he did not die, and for that he will pray extra times in gratitude. He then explains: As he was coming home he got a flat tire, so he parked the truck on the side of the road. He was only half a mile away, but he thought that because of the rain and fog and the lack of streetlights, it would be unwise to leave the truck there for the night. Other cars could easily crash into it, risking someone's life. So he raised it up on a jack to fix the tire. He had done this many times before. But because of the mud, the jack slipped, and the truck fell onto his thumb and severed it.

Without thinking, and before the shocking pain overtook

him, he picked up the piece of his thumb and pressed it back to where it was before. He then ran and walked in the storm, sometimes silent, sometimes howling his pain, until he got home.

"*Behyat rabbak*, by the name of Allah, find a different kind of job," Mother pleads once again when Father is ready to go back to work. He resists at first because he does not want to hear such talk, but then he finds a job as a school guard. He sticks with it for a few weeks, then quits because when he falls asleep the boys sneak out through the school gate. He cannot wake up to stop them, and he feels ashamed and humiliated when the teachers see this.

At home, he bangs his fists on the wall in impatience, angry tears in his eyes. And he grieves that in losing part of his thumb he lost part of his fingerprint, his identity. When letting himself feel this loss, he also finds himself remembering how much he misses a world that his thumb once touched: his mother's face, his father's hands—both of whom are dead—his many relatives whom he does not see because borders are closed.

As Father battles his demons, it is getting closer to the time when Mother will have the baby. Father still cannot find a job that doesn't involve driving, so the upcoming birth adds to his worries, and rather than cheering him it makes him feel sad and burdened.

He tells Mother that he will not borrow money from anyone

to pay for the birth expenses. So he goes back to being a truck driver.

Mother disagrees strongly, urging him to have hope that he can find work that does not put his life in danger every day.

"Driving is my destiny," he shouts at her.

One night they argue so loudly that I am sure all the neighbors must hear them. Then Father turns against himself. As we watch, he takes off a shoe and hits himself repeatedly on the head with it. We look at one another in astonishment as he explains that he is punishing himself for not knowing how to solve his problems.

Father then confesses that his soul is wrestling with him about whether to leave or stay, filling him with an anguish he cannot bear. He says that he is tortured and announces that his soul no longer wants to live in the pain of his mind and body; it wants to grab his last breath and leave forever.

We gaze at him, not knowing what he means. But the next day he tells us.

Despair

"I want to die," Father says after he comes home early from work. We are speechless as he continues. "Day and night, I worry about having an accident. And it is not because I fear death. On the contrary, I welcome its great relief." He flings his arms high. "I am tormented about leaving all of you with no one to support or protect you in this merciless world." He pulls the keys for the truck from his pocket and shakes them nervously. "But God, who understands that I face unbearable daily battles, and that I'm too weary to go on, will forgive me." He turns to leave.

Now we understand that Father is saying goodbye to us. There is complete silence in the room before we all say that we will go with him anywhere in life, in death, in the afterlife, or any other place. We run to put on our jackets and shoes.

We are all talking at the same time. If Allah finds that Father was wrong to do this and sends him to hell, we can go there, too, as one family. We can tell Allah that we wanted to die with Father, that we prefer to go together, just as we did when we fled the stone house in the Six-Day War. But now we flee to God.

Father shakes his head and silently walks to the truck. He is determined. Mother makes sure that everything in the apartment is neatly in place. She does not want people who will see our apartment later on to say that she was a messy housekeeper. Such words would be harsher than death for her, and would make her unhappy all the way from Ramallah to the afterlife. When she is satisfied, she wobbles out and gets into the truck next to Father. Mona helps Samer climb up, and they sit on opposite sides of Mother's pregnant belly.

Basel, Muhammad, and I ride on the bed of the truck. Now a strange feeling of happiness fills the world. We are going to end all our problems at once and never be separated from one another.

As we leave the city behind, Father waves goodbye to the drivers of the cars we pass. They wave back. When Father reaches the empty winding roads where there aren't even shepherds tending goats on the surrounding hills, he begins to speed up.

Basel, Muhammad, and I respond by jumping up and down on the bed of the truck, which is now bouncing like a trampoline under us. We try to jump higher and higher. We lose our balance, fall down, then get up to play again. When we spot a roll of toilet paper inside a tub of tools, we unfurl it in the wind to create a long tail for the speeding truck. The toilet paper strip gets longer and longer and ripples in the wind. We sing and laugh ecstatically.

Father starts to press harder on the gas pedal, and Mother begins to ask him to stop. *"Suleiman!"* She shouts father's name. *"Waqqef! Waqqef!"* Stop! Stop! My parents are speaking faster than the speeding truck, and their words come out of the open windows and reach us.

But nothing matters to Basel, Muhammad, and me. One thing is on our minds: we do not want Father to die alone and for us to be left behind. Now we are saying our prayers and letting go of the scenes behind us.

Father continues to drive faster and faster. I think that the truck will veer off the road and be destroyed, and then the angels that know Father from helping him when he sleeps will come and pick us up and take us to heaven. The toilet paper roll has nothing left now except the cardboard piece, which we use as a microphone to magnify our final words.

Suddenly, the truck comes to a stop. Father turns off the engine, and my parents get out and walk to a field. They continue their tense exchange of words, and their bodies speak, too, leaning and turning, their hands waving in the air. It is like they are dancing their high-pitched conversation, questions and answers, around each other.

When they return, sweat is rolling down their faces and they are strangely quiet. Father's face is soft, as if he had never been angry. He starts the truck and drives slowly and carefully, which is not as exciting for us as the fast driving. When we reach a small town, he parks near a falafel shop. The owner is a friend of his. He sees how exhausted Father is, so he gives us sandwiches and sodas. "On me!" he announces when Father wants to pay. Later we go home feeling closer to Father and to one another than ever before.

"What happened?" I ask Mother the next day.

"Because we showed him that we loved him so much, that we would die with him, it made him want to live again," she says. "But let us forget that it ever happened."

Although no one speaks of that event, I continue to think about it. And I dream of a time in the future when I can work so that Father does not have to pay for my expenses, and when I have enough money, I will buy him all that he likes. He can sleep, eat, have a goat, and sing to it all day.

Soon after, Mother gives birth to my brother Najm, the fourth boy in our family. During the forty days following his birth, the special period of time for women to recover after giving birth, Grandma Fatima comes to help out often and our house fills with women bringing baby clothes, sky-blue blankets, chocolate, stories, and words of congratulations.

We use the candy that people bring us to offer as treats to the people who come after them. Mother saves most of the baby clothes she is given unopened in the packages so she does not have to buy presents in the future when visiting friends and relatives with their own newborns.

When the women look at me and pay the customary compliment of wishing for my marriage day, Mother firmly objects: "Why wish the unhappiness of early marriage on her?" That makes me think that Mother is not happy that she married Father when she was just fifteen. The women quickly change the subject.

Father's sister, Aunt Rasmeyyah, comes to visit from Jerusalem. She mentions that one of her sons wants to ask for my hand in marriage and will wait until I finish high school if necessary. Today she is only checking to see if my parents would agree. Mother lets me answer. I reply that my aunt's son has his own two hands; why does he need mine? I need both of my hands and will not give them to anyone.

Mother then points to me and says, "Is this an answer from someone who should be thinking of marriage? She is only eight years old, too young to even know what you mean."

"There is no problem in asking," Aunt Rasmeyyah chastises. "The Prophet Muhammad married a young girl."

"That was over thirteen hundred years ago," Mother shoots back. "And when your son becomes a prophet, we can reconsider." She smiles and my aunt smiles, too, but promises to ask again in the future.

I go to watch the men who are here to congratulate us on the birth. They sit outside with Father and speak about work, land, politics, religion, children, past and present wars, and the latest operations of armed resistance by the fedayeen. The resistance gives Father and the men hope that living under the occupation may not be forever.

Among the guests is Father's friend Abu Qassem. After he sees Father's thumb, he offers him a job in his business to spare him the risk of being on the road. Father agrees to try because he knows that it would please Mother.

Abu Qassem's business, however, is nothing more than a wooden cart a few feet long and a few feet wide. It is piled up with a myriad of random items: children's clothes, plates, plastic cups, aluminum colanders, baby shoes, hair combs and clips, loofahs, hand mirrors, whistles, boxes of matches, batteries, and so on.

The cart is parked every day at the edge of the main *hesbeh*, the farmers' market, near the Upper Ramallah central bus station. Thousands of people come through the station every morning and afternoon on their way to and from work. Rows of vendors are parked there, and shoppers stand in lines for the carts as much as they stand in lines for the buses.

A few weeks into the new job with Abu Qassem, Father tells us that he falls asleep at this job, too, but wakes up quickly because the buses make loud noises coming and going, and the farmers and vendors shout most of the time as they sell their goods.

A whole year passes like the shadow of a speeding cloud. I am almost done with the fourth grade when Mother becomes pregnant again. I am wondering if she will become like Aunt Amina, whom we've heard just had her eleventh girl. But Mother tells everyone this will be her last child.

I am happy to hear this because having more boys adds to my chores. Most Palestinian families, such as ours, do not ask boys to do any housework. Girls cook, mop the floors, wash dishes, do laundry, fold the clothes, clean windows, and organize the house while the boys either run errands or have jobs outside, or play sports and spend a lot of time with their friends.

I think my job in the family should be to do only one-sixth of the work, my exact share, and then I should be allowed to play like a boy. When I grow up and am free, I promise myself I will not wash even one dish.

Over the past year, we had all begun to think that Father had finally found the right job, but he announces that one year of working at Abu Qassem's cart is enough.

"Every time I see the buses and drivers coming and going, while I am standing in one place all day arguing with old and young women about prices, the feeling of loss crushes me," he complains. "When I drove, I felt the freedom of seeing open fields, sunrises, sunsets, wild animals, the change of seasons, forests of olive trees, groves of orange trees, and I was in constant prayer for Allah to help me with my sleeping plight. As I drove, I even forgot that the land had become contested. No one can contest the fragrance of citrus groves in Tūlkarm, or the celestial yellow of the banana groves of Jericho."

Abu Qassem and Father have known each other for a long time, so they part in business but remain close friends. Quickly, Father finds what he hoped for: an owner of a truck who needs a driver to deliver produce. Father can begin work in one month, and he will go all over the West Bank, to Jerusalem and many other cities again, but he cannot keep the truck in Ramallah at night. It is to be parked in the nearby town of Beitunia, where the owner of the truck lives. For that job, our family must move again. If we move to Beitunia, within a few blocks of the owner's house, Father can keep the truck at night, too, and if he pays for the extra fuel, he can use it for the move and for other family needs.

When I go to see Um Ibrahim for the last time, she piles up so much ice cream for me that I have to ask her to stop. She then asks if I am still sure the baby Mother is going to have will be a boy. I say that I am certain because Allah likes my father and answers his prayers or else Father would have been dead a long time ago.

Haj Hamd Allah watches from his glass veranda as we leave for Beitunia. He has the same expression he always has when he looks at people going and coming. I am surprised that I have the same feeling I had when we left the stone house—wanting to cry on the inside because I'm losing my home, and happy that I have many memories I can take with me.

PART II

Beitunia
1973–1975

Belonging

Beitunia is profuse with apricot, plum, and pear orchards, but the only people we see on the main road are two old men sitting under a gazebo covered in grapevines in front of a shop we pass. The sign on the store says SUPERMARKET in both English and Arabic. The two men are dressed in the traditional *qumbaz*, the Palestinian costume that is like a woman's dress and goes all the way to their ankles. They also wear the *hatta wa egal*, the traditional headdress that my father wears. They are leaning over a small table playing dice.

One minute past them, we enter a long driveway that climbs up and up and park in front of a tall building. "An *elleyyah*, a summer vacation house," Mother exclaims. "Even Haj Hamd Allah would want to live here."

"But the town is so empty, everyone must be on vacation," Basel says.

Father explains that most of the original residents of Beitunia have migrated to North and South America, and that is why we can have a spacious apartment for a low rent compared to the prices in Ramallah.

The roof of our new house is covered with Spanish tiles that absorb the hot sunlight. The sign carved in stone above the entrance reads: AL-MULKU LE-ALLAH, all things belong to Allah, next to the date when the house was built.

The front yard is the size of a school playground; my brothers can kick soccer balls with all their might without breaking anyone's windows. The backyard is filled with trees like a lush small forest, including a giant fig tree with sturdy climbable branches and hundreds of fruits shaped like little money purses, promising a taste so sweet birds will compete with me for them. Father also likes fig trees, but for a different reason. For him it is because in the Qur'an God honors this timeless tree as sacred, ranking it even above the olive tree.

Standing near the heavy iron front door of the *elleyyah*, I think that the house has been erected not as a summer vacation house but as a fort. The door needs a five-inch-long key to open it, and with each turn the key hitting the bolt sounds like a gunshot. Entering, we discover that separating this door from our apartment upstairs is a staircase of forty-five steps. My siblings and I instantly begin a competition jumping up and down them. But pregnant Mother must sit on the steps to rest, and then lean on the wall as she climbs. Inside the apartment, the ceilings are so high we will not be able to clean cobwebs from the corners of the rooms because we do not have a ladder tall enough to reach them.

The many windows allow the sun to pour in like rivers of light. On the floor, the tiles are hand-painted mosaic squares of geometric shapes in green, beige, and burgundy.

At night, because we are on the second floor, we do not have to close the windows for safety. And when the lights are out, instead of going to sleep immediately, I sit on my mattress and gaze through the windows at the moon and the stars. I remember a song called "Nehna Wel Amar Jeeran" (We are neighbors of the moon) and feel that our house is not only a neighbor of the moon but also a friend. In the basement apartment, I had missed seeing the big night sky.

Another special advantage of this new apartment is that we are almost at the height of the Beitunia mosque's minaret, the tall tower that makes the mosque look like a lighthouse. So when I hear the *athan*, the Islamic call to prayer, which is recited from the loudspeaker of every mosque's minaret five times a day, every day of the year, the words are clear, as though recited not from across town but from the fig tree.

I have always liked the *athan* because it makes me feel that I am connected to everything around me. Perhaps it is because Father prayed the *athan* in my right ear when I was born, exactly like I saw him do with Najm last year. He held Najm and said the words so that Najm would feel at home when hearing the *athan*. And each time Najm hears it, his spirit will open up for hope and learning. Father said it is a tradition in Muslim families for one of the parents or a relative to say this prayer into the ears of a newborn.

At the end of the summer, my parents decide that Basel and Muhammad will continue their schooling in Ramallah, but will move from the Jalazone Boys' School to another UNRWA boys' school closer to Beitunia. They will take the bus back and forth every day. Mona and I will walk to Beitunia Girls' School at the farthest end of the town. It is a combined elementary and middle school, with classes from first through ninth grade.

I am excited about starting fifth grade because that is the year when English is compulsory in all Palestinian public schools. Every day we study English for forty-five minutes, but I study on my own for hours, always adding any new English word I learn to the Arabic sentences I speak: *Ana* live *fee Beitunia*, meaning: I live in Beitunia. *Al-sama'* blue: the sky is blue. When people don't understand the mixed languages and say, "*Shoo?* What?," that is my chance to explain to them and practice my learning more and more.

Mona and I try to speak to our new schoolmates and get to know them, but we have little in common. Many are wealthy in ways to which we cannot relate: one girl's family owns the bus company, another girl's family owns the house we live in and other buildings in Beitunia, and a third's father is the *mukhtar*, the elder of the town. Beitunia's school is funded by

Palestinians who used to live here but now live abroad. Spacious and clean, it has everything, including a small theater.

Most of the girls wear brand-new clothes and shoes, and they have schoolbags and school supplies from different countries, such as Canada, Venezuela, Chile, and Brazil. They have money to buy treats from the school canteen. There are many different colors of chalk in our classrooms, and no one takes it home. If this were my old school, not even the colored chalk dust would stay.

It is hard not to feel ashamed of having so little compared to my classmates. Mother notices this and tells me that money comes and goes but learning comes and makes one go forward with it. "But why doesn't more money come to us?" I ask. She remains quiet.

I then beg Mother for a lira, the paper money we use. She refuses. I explain to her that I only want to draw it in my notebook, not spend it.

"All right, for a few minutes," she agrees.

So I draw the one lira many times on many pages, making it ten times the amount by adding a zero, then one hundred, then one thousand. I offer her the notebook as I return the lira. That makes her laugh, which makes me feel that I made her happy for one minute. That minute will make me happy for a whole day. Among the many classes I wish I could add to my studies is a class about how to make Mother happy without my having to stop doing the things I love to do.

Because I want to make friends so that the Beitunia Girls' School will begin to feel like it is mine, too, I listen to what my classmates talk about as we walk home and learn about their world. But for days, all they do is gossip about people.

Do you think he will talk to her tomorrow? Did she explain to him about her father? They traveled without letting anyone know. She is more attractive than her cousin. I am annoyed because I have no idea whom and what they are discussing. So I decide that they must be speaking about their relatives who live in other countries.

But finally, Hoda, the town elder's daughter, notices my confusion and says that these are actors in the Egyptian soap operas she and my classmates watch every evening on television. Now I see the problem: we do not own a television set. So I walk home with tears in my eyes as I begin to understand the purpose of the many antennas on the roofs. I am feeling ashamed and deprived: What else do they see that I do not know about? I can participate in none of their conversations.

I decide to talk to two of my teachers about this. When I speak to them I use the title *Sitt*, meaning lady, as I do with all female teachers. My math teacher, Sitt Ikram, and my Arabic teacher, Sitt Adalah, both encourage me to ignore television. Sitt Ikram assures me that there will be no questions from the "foolish soap operas" on her exams. And Sitt Adalah says, "Show them good grades and they will come to you wanting to be your friends." I am happy with my teachers' comments but still want to watch those soap operas if I can.

School is easy for me because I have learned every subject

one or two years ahead of my class, from my older brothers. When Muhammad does his homework, I sit next to him and ask him to teach me as though I am his student. He loves reading out loud and especially loves to tell me when I am wrong. We compete in learning, and that makes me progress more.

Basel is reading *Around the World in Eighty Days* for school, and he excitedly translates sentences and speaks of the fictitious British character Mr. Phileas Fogg as though he were entirely real.

I copy all the new English words I learn from school and from *Around the World in Eighty Days* on scraps of paper and deposit them with their meanings inside a small toy bank. The bank has no money—only pieces of paper that I fold and deposit into it. This is my word wealth, and I plan to add to it daily so that I will have more language knowledge than my classmates have money.

Ramadan

Mother gives birth to my fifth brother, Jamal, shortly after school starts. His name means beauty. All I want to do is carry him, look at his face, and speak to him. I don't want to leave him for even a minute.

Jamal opens his cinnamon-brown eyes for a short time, then closes them. I rock him and speak to him in two languages: "Our family's name is Barakat, an Arabic word that means blessings. You were born on al-Sabt, Saturday. Today is al-Ethnayn, Monday, your first Monday as a newborn on the planet. Our planet's name is Ard, Earth. Can you believe that the *ard* is spinning like a top all the time? Tomorrow has two names: Tuesday and the future. Our family uses two different calendars: one is lunar and tells the years that have passed since the beginning of Islam, and the other is called the solar Christian calendar because it honors the history of Christianity. The

Islamic calendar says this year is 1393; the solar calendar says this year is 1973. They are different because the religion of Islam is a younger sibling of Christianity, and the lunar year is shorter than the solar year by ten or eleven days. I hope that you will grow up to love languages and mathematics like I do."

When I think he is ready for more, I hold him up to the night sky. *Would you like to sit inside the scoop of the Big Dipper? Or do you want the Little Dipper? I can make a hammock for you between them and rock you to sleep.*

When Jamal is almost two weeks old, the monthlong celebration of Ramadan begins. It is the time of the year when Muslims abstain from food and drink all day long. Unlike in other months of the year, the *iftar* meal, breakfast, is served at the end of the day, not the beginning. A fasting person also cannot chew gum or smoke.

Ramadan is the lunar month of the ancient Arabic calendar when the Prophet Muhammad went to sit alone inside a desert cave called Hira' in the country now known as Saudi Arabia. He meditated and listened to the Archangel Gabriel reveal verses of the Qur'an, the holy scriptures of Islam. The revelation of the Qur'an during Ramadan made this month sacred for the Arab people who became followers of the Prophet Muhammad. After the formation of Islam, Muslims took the date of the Prophet Muhammad's migration from Mecca, his hometown, to Yathrib, another town more than two hundred fifty miles north of Mecca where Islam spread quickly, to be the beginning of the Muslim calendar, 1,393 lunar years ago.

Muslim children do not have to fast during Ramadan. My parents say we will do so when we are older. Mother is also excused from fasting during this Ramadan because of the recent birth. When nursing, sick, weak, or traveling, a Muslim does not need to fast, but does have to make up for that by giving alms or by fasting for the number of missed Ramadan days in another month.

During Ramadan, Father wakes up at three-thirty or four in the morning for the *suhur*, the special small meal a Muslim can have before sunrise that makes it possible to endure hunger and especially thirst for fourteen or fifteen hours. Father does not need an alarm clock to wake up. He also never falls asleep during prayer, but sometimes he weeps quietly during this time devoted to Allah. We know this because we can hear him, and after prayer we see his tearful eyes.

There is also a *musahher*, a man who carries a drum and a stick, who helps wake those who want to eat *suhur*. A *musahher* exists in every city and village where Ramadan is celebrated. He starts his work at three-thirty in the morning and goes from door to door beating on a drum under people's bedroom windows, saying, *Ya nayem, wahhed al-dayem*. You who are asleep, wake up and worship God the Everlasting. As the *musahher* walks along the street, lights come on in one house after another. It is as though his drumstick is a light switch.

The *mu'athen*, the man who recites the *athan* at the minaret, also helps wake people during Ramadan by reading over the mosque's loudspeaker verses from the Qur'an that praise the ritual of fasting. Then he calls the *athan* at the highest pitch of his voice, to reach ears as far as possible and mark the first light of dawn, which is the exact moment people must stop eating and drinking.

Because my siblings and I don't fast, Father emphasizes that it is not only food that one must set aside during Ramadan but also words, thoughts, or actions that are harmful to oneself or others. He tells us endless facts about Islam. I am eager to learn and I especially love when he says that each year, beginning about two months after Ramadan, and for one-third of the year, Muslims must avoid fighting with anyone or hunting and killing any animals. These peaceful four months are called the *ashhur al-hurum*, the sacred months.

While observing Ramadan, many people work only in the morning, and rest or sleep during the afternoon. The school day becomes shorter because our teachers, all women, need to go home early to prepare meals. Every evening, *iftar* is preceded by great excitement as we count down minute by minute, then second by second, until the sun sets and we can eat. I hold my wooden ruler against the window and measure how far the sun has to travel to reach the horizon line and disappear.

While we set the table for *iftar*, we listen to a radio program hosted by the religious journalist Abu Jareer, who chants *thekr*, the Islamic rhymed blessings that, when repeated over and over, can bring spiritual gratitude. Abu Jareer leads, and we murmur the words after him. When it is finally time to eat, his voice swells up with joy as he announces: *"Hana al'an mawa'ed al-iftar.*" It is now time to break the fast. Those words put the biggest smiles on our faces.

We call this announcement the *sawt al-madfaa'*, the sound of the cannon. There is no real cannon, only the name. My parents explained that in the past, before radios made it possible for information to reach everyone at the same time, a blast fired from a cannon alerted everyone far and near to begin eating.

But then on October 6, while we are continuing to celebrate Ramadan and the Israelis are having their Yom Kippur observance, to our great surprise and horror, we hear real cannons. We do not want to believe we are hearing the dreaded sounds of war. But they are outside and also on the radio.

Egypt has attacked the Israeli border, wanting to regain control over the Egyptian Sinai Desert and the Suez Canal, which were occupied by Israel after the Six-Day War. Israel built a defense line called the Bar-Lev to separate Egypt from the Egyptian areas Israel had gained. The Syrian Golan Heights border was also occupied by Israel as a result of the Six-Day War, so Syria is part of today's attack, aiming to break the Israeli hold there.

Father estimates that it is not more than a hundred and fifty miles between where we live and the front line in the Syrian Golan Heights. He is hopeful that Egypt and Syria will be successful against the Israelis because their victory may mean liberation for us. As he speaks, we hear sirens.

Mother begins packing our belongings. "War has a way of

displacing people in the blink of an eye, and we must be ready to go," she laments.

"I feel afraid," I tell Mother.

She shouts that she does not want to hear it. "Feel something else!"

Now I want to open my schoolbag and hide inside it, nestle between the covers of books, enter other worlds and stories. I quietly put on my shoes and place my schoolbag where I can see it. I busy myself by gently swinging Jamal's bassinet so he will not cry and make Mother more agitated. I give Najm a ball he likes to play with, and he chases it around the room.

Muhammad goes to the kitchen and eats and eats. That is what he does when he feels anxious. Basel becomes quiet. He does not answer if anyone asks him a question. If pressed, he becomes angry. Mona puts on many layers of clothes and a coat and says that she now feels safe. Samer holds hands with Father and becomes part of him. Father becomes one with the radio.

The next morning, the announcer on the Egyptian radio bellows news of victory. "Six hours, not six days," he cheers. He explains that the Egyptian army broke the Israeli Bar-Lev defense line on the edge of the Sinai Desert and crossed the Suez Canal. War songs fill the airwaves and resemble desperate calls for prayer, saying *bessm ellah*, in the name of Allah, victory will grow. The radio also airs sound tracks of the battlefield to encourage the Egyptian troops to press on and liberate more of the Sinai Desert.

People in Beitunia gather on the streets with their handheld radios. Some say they have not felt happy since the Nakba in 1948 and this Egyptian victory stirs hope in their hearts. Others say that, since the Six-Day War, they had feared that Arabs could not defeat the Israeli army—and now they are celebrating because that fear is gone. Everyone prays that the Egyptian army will soon liberate the Sinai Desert from Israeli occupation and move on to the Gaza Strip and us.

But soon we hear on the radio that the United States will send massive military support to Israel. So the news shifts to the actions of the big powers and their role in our lives: the US military support of Israel on the one hand and the Soviet Union's military support of Arabs on the other.

Ramadan amid war becomes a mix of food words and war words: *shorabat khudar*, vegetable soup; *atayef*, nut-stuffed half-moons; *qamar al-din*, dried apricots with pine nuts; Khat Bar-Lev, the Bar-Lev armistice line; Qanat al-Suais, the Suez Canal; and Ta'erat MiG Wahed Wa Aashreen, Russian-made MiG-21 fighters that are battling US-made Skyhawk fighter planes.

Then the main oil-producing Arab countries begin to withhold their petroleum exports to the United States and several other countries as retaliation for their political stance on the events. They hope to create economic pressure and shift the outcome of the war in favor of Egypt and Syria. Kerosene and gas prices go up and make it necessary for us to ration our fuel.

I become like the grownups, obsessed with news. A ceasefire is enforced within weeks, but the oil embargo and political fighting continue for months after Ramadan and are the primary theme of the news. The Egyptian radio endlessly repeats the special songs aired during Egypt's initial victories.

Even though it is now clear that Egypt will not liberate us from the Israeli occupation, Mother hums along with the victory songs as she does housework. "*Tahya Masr.* Long live Egypt," she sings. Father sings along with her.

The soap operas are less important to my classmates now that war and months of political reports have changed the focus of our lives. So my friendships with them become stronger and I learn more about them.

Wafa, who lives only two houses away, likes to walk slowly, as though she does not want to arrive at school in the morning or arrive at home in the afternoon. She says that her mother is sick, which leaves her with much housework.

Zaina is the only brown-skinned girl at school. Mother has warned me and Mona that if we sit in the sun too long our skin will become dark and that will affect how people respond to us. She says many men prefer to marry light-skinned women. So I ask Zaina if her mother has not explained she should not sit in the sun, but she says it is not a tan, her skin is naturally this color. And so is her mother's. She invites me to visit her home and meet her family, which I do.

When Hoda, the daughter of the town elder, speaks to me, she constantly adjusts her padded bra under her school dress. I do not wear a bra because I am still flat as a book. She also mentions that she has her period. I have no idea what she means. She says that even though we are in the same grade, she is two years older than me. She is my brother Muhammad's age. Muhammad is one grade ahead of me, instead of two, because when it was time for him to start first grade, our family was in Jordan awaiting permission to return to Ramallah after the Six-Day War, so he lost a school year. I wonder what happened to Hoda and to all the other girls in my school during that war.

When I start sixth grade, I decide to try to make friends with the middle school students in the seventh, eighth, and ninth grades. I stand at the sidelines of their volleyball games and bring back their stray balls. The older girls start to treat me like a younger sister, tying my undone hair ribbon or patting my shoulder to acknowledge that they like me.

Their warmth makes me feel more and more at home at Beitunia Girls' School and encourages me to participate in more activities. I am especially looking forward to when our school will have a cultural costume pageant called Children of the World and perform a special play that one of the teachers wrote with the ninth-grade students, about war. Those who are chosen to participate will get extra credit.

My goal is to get a chance to stand on stage for the first time and speak to a crowd of people whose only task for those minutes is to listen to me. I anticipate that it will be close to the pleasure of calling the *athan*, an experience I will never know. In Islam, girls and women are not allowed to perform the call to prayer. We are also not supposed to sing in public, although many Arab women defy that religious teaching, singing in public about love and longing. But I have not ever heard of a woman calling the *athan*. So I whisper it to myself and imagine it amplified a thousand times.

Even though I don't know whether I will be selected to participate in the pageant or the play, I practice. I stand at the top of our forty-five steps, or on an empty chair in the house, or on the stacked-up *farshaat*, mattresses, that we fold in the morning and unfold at night, and make speeches. "To you, dear *farshaat*, that help us sleep and hold many of our night dreams, the residents of this house offer thanks."

I grow more and more eager for the auditions and happily count down to them like I count down to the sunset preceding a Ramadan dinner. Finally they arrive, but they begin with sadness.

Death

I know Wafa is excited about today's auditions, too. I go to her house and call her name, expecting that she will run out like she does every day, her big white ribbon flying behind her on her ponytail. But Wafa does not answer. I call again. Nothing. I think she must have overslept.

I throw a pebble at the green metal shutters on her window, and when she still doesn't come out I knock on the front door. I hear slow footsteps, and when Wafa opens it her face is pale and her eyes are teary. She says her mother died last night. Preparations are being made to bury her within twenty-four hours, the custom in Islam.

Twenty-four hours and she will never see or touch her mother again. I cannot grasp the thought. That is only 1,440 minutes. Before I say another word, one minute of that will be gone. I embrace Wafa, sharing her tears. What do people say when hearing such news? I search for the right words, but all I can think is that now two minutes are gone.

"I can bring you notes from all our classes," I finally offer.

She is quiet, then answers in a stumbling voice: "*Ma fee hajeh,* no need. My family has decided to take me out of school." She explains that they need her to stay home to run the household.

I want to shout: *That is wrong; do not let them do it!* I want to tell Wafa to come and see my mother, how unhappy she is because she was taken out of school after the sixth grade. But I say nothing. Instead, I embrace her again, and as I walk away, I wonder whether I should run to school or run home to see my mother's face and touch her hand.

For three days after the death of Wafa's mother, mourners enter and leave her house, all wearing black. Some are carrying *aaseedah*, the unsweetened whole-wheat meal people prepare to console those grieving a death. It is meant to be a heavy meal, to replace the strange and aching hunger for food that strikes many people when someone dies.

When I see Wafa again, she appears to have accepted her destiny but asks that I still visit and tell her the news of the school. I am not certain whether this will make her feel sad or will help her feel connected to everyone. I mention that the auditions took place and she wants to know all about them. I tell her I got the role of a Korean girl for the pageant, and was also cast as a boy in the play about war. The lead in the play, a ninth-grade girl named Amal, who is from the volleyball team, said I would be the right choice.

Wafa then wants to know which of our other classmates were selected and what roles they got. I tell her all that I remember.

Most of my time outside of school I pretend I'm on stage at a theater. Now, instead of the stairs and mattresses, I climb to a high branch of the fig tree and speak to the leaves as if they are my audience. When they shake in the wind I think they find what I say moving. The birds stop singing and look on with interest. "Now you can take a break from singing all day, sit back, and be entertained," I tell them before I start singing to them.

During the pageant I will wear a Korean *hanbok*, a dress with a big underskirt that opens like an upside-down flower. An outer skirt wraps around the dress with straps. A long cloth belt ties in the back in the shape of a butterfly and reaches the floor. I will have a jacket and a small black tulle cap with flowers on it. My costume is beautiful.

After greeting the audience with a bow, I will tell them that I am a girl from Korea and ask them to imagine going there with me. It is in Asia like we are, but it is completely different. Detail by detail I will present Korea's social customs, music, food, and culture. Even though I've never eaten rice with chopsticks and my teachers can't tell me how it is done, my dream is to speak so well that everyone in the audience will feel Korean during my performance.

On the day of the show, the actors gather backstage to get

ready. On the wall is a big map of the world colored to identify the countries we are representing. They are all on the map—except for Palestine. Although no one speaks of this, when we happily touch the countries we are representing, we also press our fingers on the place where Palestine once was on the map, with sadness.

We put on our costumes. We usually don't wear makeup but are allowed to today so that we will appear dramatic on stage. Voices call asking for help with zippers or buttons or hairdos. Bobby pins are everywhere. Teachers are going from girl to girl addressing us by our country names, then listening to each of us rehearse our words.

"Unless it's part of the role, smiling or laughing on the stage spoils the effect of the performance," the teacher who directs the show emphasizes for the hundredth time. I really want to smile though, because many people will have cameras. But I will do exactly what she asks.

Finally, we are all ready. The teacher managing the stage entrance whispers: "Now." The audience begins to clap as we enter and line up on stage. There is more clapping after each girl transports the audience to her country: Canada, Russia, Morocco, Spain, Yemen, the United States of America, Brazil, Nigeria, France, Algeria, India, Australia, and others. At the end, we shout, "We are children of the world. We wish the world would listen to children and what they have to say." Some people in the audience shout, "Yes," but others laugh, perhaps dismissing our message as childish.

We all go backstage. The play will be next. A teacher recites a poem to the audience while I quickly change into my boy costume: I am a soldier who says goodbye to his mother before going to war. The teachers gather around to help me get ready.

I put on a khaki shirt that I borrowed from my father. It reaches below my knees. One teacher is fumbling to find the buttons. Another is helping with a pair of big boots. A third is slinging a long green ruler threaded with a string over my shoulder—it is supposed to represent a gun. Then they wrap my head with the white-and-black Palestinian *kufiyyah*. I have never felt this much like a boy.

Amal was cast as my mother, and she enters the stage first, wearing an old woman's Palestinian garments. She begins by speaking to herself and pacing like a parent who is not certain what will happen to her son. The audience is silent as they listen to her.

"Ready?" The teacher who manages the stage entrance gently puts her hand on my shoulder. I nod excitedly.

At her signal, I take a deep breath and walk slowly on stage, my boots making a loud noise like a war drum against the wood. I look at Amal's eyes. They are red with sorrow. I reach where she is sitting and sit beside her. We gaze at each other and then embrace.

I begin speaking to Amal like I am one of the soldiers whose actions are reported on the news for the world to know: "Mother, it is time for me to go to battle. All I want is that we live in freedom, but freedom is never given without risking one's life for it. Please forgive me if I do not come back."

I say my lines exactly as instructed by the teacher who directed the play. "Words are music," she had said. "There are many ways to say each sentence, and each takes the listener to a different place. Not one *ah* different from what I taught you!"

When I am done, the audience cheers and whistles. Then Amal touches my face and moves my scarf to the side to kiss my cheeks and say goodbye. Her eyes fill with tears that never happened during rehearsals. I am moved to great sadness with her.

When I walk backstage I can't stop crying. I sit in a dark corner and, with everyone else, listen to her sing of her desire to see her son live. She then begins to chant her words, repeating them over and over.

People in the audience join her, adding their desire for life to hers, and when she's done, everyone shouts bravo and stands up to clap. I run back on stage and hold her hand as we do a final bow.

Mother is in the front row and she is standing, too. I am happy that I did not disappoint her. She can turn to the other women and say: *That brave boy on stage is my daughter!*

At home, I am glad that I am not going to any war, and will live. But thoughts of death are hard to push away.

I think of Wafa and imagine how it must feel when your mother dies, leaving you behind. I also wonder whether it is possible to have freedom without death and fighting. I remember the Ramadan war. All the mothers of all the soldiers who fought must have felt like Amal. The Israeli soldiers who trained outside our stone house on the hill also come to mind. Do their mothers feel the same way?

Toward the end of the school year, Hoda tells me that she is engaged to be married. Her wedding will be in two weeks and her honeymoon will be in Honolulu. I don't know where that is, but Hoda says it is a place that has big flowers and no wars at all. She is happy to be getting married and leaving home.

When I tell Mother about Hoda's plans, she replies that Hoda will most likely not have a honeymoon. "What honey?" She shakes her head. "She will probably have a *maqloobeh* moon, because from day one, she will find herself having to cook the *maqloobeh* traditional meal, clean house from morning to evening, and then have children and raise them, even though she is a child herself."

I shake my head and say nothing, because Mother loves to be critical and speak as though she knows everything. I hope that Hoda will have a honey week at least.

I go to Hoda's wedding to thank her for her friendship and for talking with me when I felt like an outsider in Beitunia. I also secretly want to see what Mother might have looked like and how she acted when she got married around this age.

I find Hoda at the center of a room, wearing a white dress

and sitting on a *loaj*, the special chair set on top of a table so all the guests can see the bride from wherever they sit or stand. People are wearing gold jewelry and new clothes and dancing around her and throwing candy at everyone.

Hoda is smiling. She has a thick coating of pink powder on her cheeks, bright red lipstick, nail polish, glitter, kohl, mascara, a fake beauty mark on her cheek, henna on her hands, and very high-heeled shoes. Her hair has been arranged into big curls that fall to her shoulders, covering half of her face. She does not push the locks aside even though they hide one of her eyes. She does not want anyone to see her smiling eyes because Palestinian brides are told not to show the families of their future husbands that they are happy to leave their parents. Many brides sit on the *loaj* with tears in their eyes for everyone to see, showing that they come from good families—families they are not eager to leave.

The wedding ends quickly because Hoda's groom did not come from America to participate. She will go to him. He will meet her on the other side of the ocean, where they will have another party. Before I leave, I want to ask her if she would send me a letter or a postcard from her new home in the United States, but I know that Hoda does not like reading and writing.

Later, looking at her empty seat in the classroom, I feel sad, but not as sad as when I discover who will be next to disappear from my world.

Red

It is a hot and quiet day in June during the summer vacation. I am recovering from seven stitches in my foot. The accident happened two weeks ago when I rode the tricycle meant for my younger brothers. My parents think that tricycles and bicycles are for boys only, and won't let me and Mona ride them.

"A girl should keep her legs together," Mother says. When I ask her why, she does not explain the reason, so I decide that if a boy can ride a bicycle I should, too. I secretly see it as close to driving a car, which I would like to do when I grow up. So anytime I find a bicycle I try to ride it. Two weeks ago, when my brothers went down to play in the yard, I found myself alone in the house with the tricycle and I jumped for joy.

Mother was outside, sitting under the shady fig tree. She was nursing Jamal in one arm and reading from her favorite book,

Al-Ard al-Tayyebah (*The Good Earth*). She must have read it twenty times. I knew that once Jamal fell asleep and she became one with the book, she would not come back into the house for a long time. She would read for as long as she could, pretending to be in China amid the fields with peasants who wear conical straw hats. I wondered if she liked the book so much because their harsh world makes her life feel easier.

So while Mother was busy, I decided to put my foot on the seat of the tricycle and push with my other foot, like a skateboard. At first, I successfully avoided all the furniture. But then, battling to not hit a cupboard filled with china in the corner of the room, I headed toward our forty-five-step staircase and rolled down. When I stopped, I had been cut by a metal edge on the tricycle that dug into my foot. I saw my skin become pink for a second, then dark purple, then red as blood poured from it.

I remembered the day I saw my father pressing his injured thumb with his hand. I pressed on my wound with all my might and shouted for help. When Mother came, she first filled the wound with coffee grounds and bandaged it; then she filled the room with damnations. I closed my eyes and ears.

As my stitches healed she called me *hassan saby*, tomboy, and kept saying, "This is the result of doing what you were told not to do."

I looked away and said to myself: *This is the result of not having the right-size bicycle.*

Today I am better but still cannot skip, jump, or run easily. My parents and siblings are shopping in Ramallah and have left me home. I thought Muhammad was with the others, but then he enters the room. He appears unhappy.

"Is everyone back already?" I ask.

"I did not go with them, and I want to tell you something that you must keep to yourself."

"*Ihkee!* Speak!"

"*Biddy ashrod,*" he confides. "I want to escape!"

"Escape to where?"

"I cannot tell you where I am going. If you don't know where, then you won't be able to tell Mother and Father and they won't be able to find me."

"Can I tell them you've left?"

"Only after I get far enough away."

He goes to the kitchen, stands on a tall chair, and urges me to hurry up next to him. I struggle to stand on the same chair, not wide enough for our four feet. So I stand on my strong foot and gaze between the tree branches to see the exact spot on the street where he is pointing.

"Right there on the edge of Beitunia. Do you see where the road intersects with cars going toward Jerusalem on the right, Ramallah on the left, and coming to Beitunia in the middle?"

"Yes."

"Stay here on the chair. It will take me twenty minutes to get there. You will be able to see me in my red jacket in the distance. When I wave to you, please wave back."

"Are you sure we will be able to see each other?"

"Yes. Look at that person passing there now. If his clothes were red, you would see him much more easily."

"Muhammad, do you not want to be my brother anymore?"

"I do. But you are a girl. Life for a boy is different."

He then mentions what happened recently when a few boys fought with him and Basel after school. When my brothers got home they said nothing. But six men related to the boys came to our house in the evening. They wouldn't stop hitting Father, so he had to jump into the truck and drive away. The following day, he had bruises everywhere.

My brothers could not protect Father. Basel regretted that he had not saved to buy a Swiss Army Knife, the only weapon a Palestinian is allowed to carry. If he had had it and waved it at the men to deter them, they might have left Father alone. Muhammad blamed himself.

"I do not want to fight with anyone," he says, "not boys or teachers or the family. I don't even want to hear on the radio about people I do not know harming one another. *Khalas*, that's it. I want a peaceful life, empty like a table that has nothing on it. I am going right now." He zips closed his bright red jacket.

"What if Mother and Father come home before you get to that spot, and ask me why with my injured foot I am standing on a chair?"

"You can make up an answer!" he says as he turns to leave.

"If you are really going to run away, take some food with you."

The cupboard is empty except for glass containers filled with flour, rice, and several kinds of dried beans and seeds. But there is also a sack of shelled almonds, and I fill his pocket. "Do not eat them all at once. I know you like to eat without stopping. And if you change your mind, come back. Our parents will be mad at you for a day for disappearing, then everything will be forgotten. They will be mad at me, too, because you told me and I didn't stop you. So we both will get into trouble together."

Muhammad leaves in a hurry. I go to get a piece of paper and a pen from my schoolbag and rush back to the kitchen, climbing up on the chair. I look into the distance. I have no watch, and our house has no wall clock, so I count to sixty for each minute, and write down the minutes as they pass. After twenty minutes I begin to wonder if Muhammad has tricked me.

He has played tricks many times before, including asking me to close my eyes and then slipping a lizard under my blouse. The lizard ran all over my body while I tumbled in a storm of terror and inconsolable cries until I saw it come out my sleeve and flicked it onto the rocks. But Muhammad's voice today, his face, his eyes, and his posture as he walked away, all tell me that he is not playing a game. If he is, I will never believe him again.

At minute thirty-two, Muhammad appears—a red dot in the late-afternoon sun. I wave frantically. He stands still and I think he waves back before walking up the street. Cars and buses come and block him for a moment, and my heart begins beating loudly until I see him again. This goes on for a few minutes until I lose him for the last time. Red, blue, green, and gray merge and bleed into the darkness of street tar, leaving me in pain as though I have just lost part of my soul. I am afraid that Muhammad is gone forever.

I get down from the chair and look around the empty apartment. I worry that Muhammad is in great danger. Mother said there are people who steal children and sell them as slaves. Soldiers might shoot at him. Bullies might hurt him. The hyenas Father told us that he feared most when he was a child might be out after dark searching for dinner.

If I were a bird, I would fly above Muhammad and know where he is going. If I were old enough and had control over things, I would not have let him go. But I control nothing other than this secret until my parents come home and I tell them.

When they get home and I explain about Muhammad, they don't know what to do. It is too late to start searching. None of us sleeps that night.

In the morning, Father goes to look for him. Day one passes. Day two follows. Muhammad does not return and Father's searches for him produce nothing. Days three and four leave my parents talking about every possibility and Father driving to different towns, asking about him. I think of Muhammad and draw red dots on paper.

It is now day five and our family is riding around in the truck, trying to find him. Father says we should look for

Muhammad in *al-khala*, the mostly uninhabited areas where only a few Bedouin families live in tents. Mother agrees.

So we drive for a long time until we see a big tent. It is pitched on land covered with green thorn bushes that have miniature tomato-red balls and pink and yellow flowers, surrounded by many hills in the distance. There are a few goats and sheep and a donkey grazing near the tent.

Outside the tent, a Bedouin man squats next to a fire pit surrounded by stones. He appears to have no cares. Father gets out of the truck and greets him. The Bedouin responds, then stands up and offers Father a tiny cup of coffee.

Sitting in the truck, we can only hear some of the conversation. But when the man says they will be back soon, we hear him clearly. The words fill us with excitement and hope.

Two boys appear within minutes, and one of them is my brother. Surprised, Muhammad looks at Father, the truck, and all of us now rushing to greet him. We embrace him, pat his hair, pretend to bite him, and tell him that he smells like a Bedouin from the pre-Islamic times who has just stepped into this century. But he is not happy to see us.

"Your son came here and asked to stay with my son, Najeh," the man explains. "They are classmates, and I know that many families are torn up by the political conditions, with many fathers who resist the occupation being arrested or disappearing, leaving behind children and wives. I didn't know about your situation, and I thank Allah that Muhammad has an intact family." He looks at us, and when we don't respond he continues: "These two boys have been doing much work to-gether. Muhammad is a hardworking boy and is sure to turn into a good man."

Father nods his head and fights for words. "It is time to come home," he finally instructs Muhammad.

"I do not want to," Muhammad replies. "I am happier here away from people, away from everything. Please let me stay and live here."

"*Ya bnayie*, my young son, you must come home with us. It is enough generosity that your friend and his father hosted you for five days."

The Bedouin man tells Muhammad to listen to Father, and Muhammad finally gets into the truck.

No blaming happens when we get home. No questioning. Muhammad is only asked to bathe and eat. My parents tell us not to talk about Muhammad's running away so that we can put it behind us. But Muhammad's return is never complete. To me, he looks like he has aged five years in those five days. He seems different, and I wonder when he'll next feel overwhelmed and decide to run away.

"Let me read you a story," I tell him as I bring a book and open it, pretending to begin. He looks on as I murmur: "What did you do and see and learn? I wished I could run away with you so you would not be alone."

He smiles. "All that time, I felt afraid, but more than fear I also felt free and strong. I wished we were still Bedouins, like the old Arabs. I learned a song that shepherds sing, smoked cigarettes, drank bitter coffee, climbed hills, milked a goat, drew on the ground with sticks, and Najeh and I made thick mustaches above our lips with cold charcoal from the fire pit and pretended to shave."

"You smoked cigarettes?"

"Yes. I even rolled one. It made me happy, and I forgot about the anxiety that fills me without my knowing why."

"Please do not continue. It smells terrible and can make you sick. You will start coughing and will not be able to run and play soccer after a while." He pretends not to hear me, so I ask, "What else happened?"

"A stray dog carried my jacket away. I ran after him and then stopped because I thought he might attack me. I watched him disappear with it. My favorite jacket! I cannot run away again without it because I cannot ask you to watch for a gray spot on the horizon."

I laugh. Then a dog barks in the distance, and to make Muhammad laugh with me I say it is the dog with the red jacket, hoping that Muhammad will give him a pair of pants to go with it.

In a few days, my parents decide it is time to move back to Ramallah. They do not want Muhammad riding the bus after school with Najeh every day, even though Najeh's father now knows that Muhammad has a family and won't let him stay overnight again. The owner of the truck Father drives lets him use it for the move. He also recommends Father to a friend of his who will give Father a new part-time driving job in Ramallah. Father will have a second job cutting stones and building houses.

Before we leave, I go to carve my name on the fig tree in the yard, but I can't bring myself to injure the trunk this way. Standing there, I remember Mother's favorite book, *The Good Earth*, which she read repeatedly under this tree. "I shall name you the Good Fig," I whisper to the tree as I embrace its trunk.

When Muhammad and I descend the forty-five steps for the last time, I tell him, "We move so often, we are like Bedouins anyway."

"By the time we graduate from high school, everyone in the country will have been our classmate or neighbor for thirty seconds," he jokes.

The minute Father drives away from Beitunia, all of us children in the back of the truck lean on the piled-up furniture and sing out loud. We look not at the road behind us, but forward to the city of Ramallah. We are going to begin the adventure of residing in the Ramallah neighborhood Ein Musbah, Spring of the Lantern. As our truck navigates the winding road toward Ein Musbah, the word *lantern* glows in my mind and I imagine I could read a book by its light. This makes me eager to get there.

PART III

Spring of the
Lantern
1975–1980

Demonstration

Our apartment in Ein Musbah is in the middle of Ramallah on top of a hill. It is on the first floor of a three-story building that is surrounded by giant houses—some of them five or six stories tall. In the afternoon, the wind blows from the valley below, where the spring is located, and creates music as it travels through the television antennas on the roofs. If Beitunia is wealthy, our street in Ein Musbah is wealthy squared or cubed.

I thank Allah that we do not have one of the big houses with many floors because that would take from morning to evening to clean.

There are also tin-roof shacks tucked around us in Ein Musbah. They look like make-believe houses built by children, but they shelter families and are hidden between the large homes. I do not know why this great contrast exists. It is as though there are many different Ramallahs.

Mona and I are happy that once again we are going to an UNRWA refugee school for girls. No one there will tease us for wearing the same shoes every day, or give us derogatory glances because our winter coats are worn out and our shabby schoolbags have holes that our pens fall through.

When Mona and I walk to school, leaving behind the affluent neighborhood, we pass a stark area with abandoned homes that belonged to people who left during wars and have never come back. The yards are overgrown and the doors are open. The buildings appear filled with mystery.

Near the abandoned houses are fenced-in homes, indicating that people live there. But the only person we ever see is a man Mona and I call the *shabah*, ghost-man. Sometimes he shouts unexpectedly from his windows and startles us as we walk by on the road. He thinks we want to trespass.

After the ghost-man's house, we pass a bakery where the aroma of freshly baked bread fills the street. The aroma quickly disappears when we cross through a big bus station full of exhaust fumes.

When we enter the central street of Ramallah al-Tahta, Lower Ramallah, with its outdoor market and shops, the air is scented with roasted pistachios, almonds, peanuts, and pumpkin and watermelon seeds. We see pyramids of herbs and spices—green thyme, burgundy sumac, golden cumin, and orange saffron. Big barrels of freshly roasted coffee make the street smell like a morning kitchen.

As we pass the small *hesbeh*, farmers' market, vendors line our path on both sides. The vendors are always singing funny lines to attract people's attention: *Asabeea al-bubu ya khyar*, cucumbers as soft as infants' fingers. *Ala al-sikkeen ya batteekh*, the knife has cut the melon; come taste before buying.

Mona and I always stop to buy an apple. Mother insists that we eat an apple a day because it "keeps the doctor away."

At the farthest end of the market is our new school, Ramallah Middle School for Girls, nicknamed Um Nader's School, after the name of its principal. It is an elementary and middle school with classes up to the ninth grade. I am starting the seventh grade and Mona is going into the fourth grade. This school is in a small house with a few extra classrooms built onto it, and has a big yard. Each grade stays in the same classroom all day and the teachers come to us.

Um Nader's School has more learning opportunities than Beitunia's, including a science club, a cooking class, a knitting club, a *dabke* folk dance group, and a beginners' music class. The school owns one small melodica and one flute, and students can take turns practicing.

The principal asks me what hobbies I have. I tell Um Nader that I like to learn everything, but if I had to choose, then I especially love sports and writing in Arabic and English. She says I can start a pen pal club in the school. That will encourage other students to begin corresponding and improve their writing skills. Our club members can choose to write in Arabic for local pen pals or use English to write internationally through a global organization in Europe.

Um Nader's school also offers me the new experience of studying with Ustaz Khaled al-Tahhan, who is the only male teacher among the school's staff of female teachers. The word *ustaz* means a male educator. Ustaz Khaled comes every day from Jerusalem to teach us science and English. Blond-haired with a light complexion reflecting his name—Tahhan, one who grinds flour—he is clever and energetic, and has a sense of humor that he occasionally mixes with a dash of mockery, enough to leave some girls in tears for the rest of the day.

Iman, who sits next to me and has green eyes and curly hair that she irons every morning as though it is a dress, spends a lot of time criticizing Ustaz Khaled. She thinks he humiliates us, and she complains that he directs all his mean comments to her in particular.

"Impossible!" I say. "He likes you as much as he likes everyone else."

"No, he does not," she says, frowning.

For several weeks, I listen closely to how Ustaz Khaled treats her to see if she is right, but in spite of what she says, I find no reason to think that he picks on her.

I decide that Ustaz Khaled acts in humorous ways mostly to entertain himself, so that he can tolerate teaching thirty-one girls who sometimes do not understand a science concept or an English grammar problem but do not say so. "All is clear and understood?" he asks. "This will be on the midyear exam." Everyone nods. He then quizzes us to see if everyone really grasped the new lesson, only to realize that many have nodded their heads to move past the question or because they are too shy to speak to a male teacher.

So in every class he paces, explaining things again, and always injecting his signature words: "*Banat*, girls—your brain, use it or lose it." He also tosses pieces of chalk from the back of the classroom over our heads, all the way to the edge of the chalkboard. If the chalk lands on the tray of the board, he celebrates as though he's made a shot in a basketball game. If it lands on someone's head, he pretends it did not happen and looks away. Some girls cry when it hits them and some giggle. Ustaz Khaled has never hit me with the chalk, but if he does I will throw it at the board and hit the tray.

I like Ustaz Khaled, and although he never shows that he favors me any more than Iman or anyone else, he often encourages me to challenge him, which I have no problem doing because, thanks to Mother, I (and my siblings) know how to talk back, argue, and fight. Mother does not want us doing this with her, but because she does it, we have learned to do it.

Ustaz Khaled likes to help our class improve in every way. When it is exam time, he tells us it is easier to remember things backward, suggesting that we start from the most recent information to the oldest when we review, not the opposite.

Regarding winter, he explains that heat leaves from our heads and ears, so he encourages us to wear hats and forget how our hair looks. About color, he tells us that green rests the eyes, so he reminds us to look often at nature.

Rumor has it that he and Sitt Wasfeyyah, our history, geography, and social sciences teacher, like each other. The girls can't stop gossiping about it.

Sitt Wasfeyyah appears shy and has a reserved smile. But she is also the school's fashion model, and every piece of clothing she wears becomes the topic of great conversation: Were too many of her shirt buttons undone? Did the charm on her necklace match her nail polish? Her earrings, her high heels, even her handwriting on the chalkboard are a source of fascination.

When we return from the midyear break, the gossip is confirmed. Ustaz Khaled and Sitt Wasfeyyah come to school together, wearing gold engagement bands.

Despite all the adoring attention he gives Sitt Wasfeyyah, and even after they marry and move their rings from their right to their left hands, Ustaz Khaled does not change the enthusiastic way he teaches us. He seems to love teaching as much as he loves Sitt Wasfeyyah.

One day in the spring he arrives in class with no books or papers. "I have a riddle," he begins. "And I am one-hundred-percent certain that only one person in this class will know the answer." We all listen to him intently as he tells the riddle: "A man came to a merchant in a money market and gave him a rare gold coin dated 500 B.C. The merchant studied the coin, flipped it back and forth noticing the minting date etched on both sides, held it in his palm to check its weight, tossed it on the ground to hear its ring, then told the man that the coin was fake, and refused to take it. How did the merchant know?"

Everyone in class raises their hands to answer, and I do, too. I also think that Ustaz Khaled is mistaken: the question is easy, and I expect half the class will know the answer.

He calls on every girl but me, and after each answer says: "Wrong." When the bell rings, he looks at me. "Ibtisam, tell them the right answer!"

"How can you know, before I speak, that my answer is going to be right?"

"Because I am a smart teacher," he says, smirking.

I give my answer: "How could the maker of the coin know that in five hundred years Jesus would be born? This is impossible. So the merchant refused the coin because no one would make coins with a date predicting an event happening half a millennium in the future."

Class is over. Ustaz Khaled concludes: "Many of you will be cheated by fake coins and false ideas if you do not start thinking harder. *Banat*, girls—your brain, use it or lose it!" He tosses a piece of chalk to the tray to emphasize his point, then leaves the classroom.

A few days later, another unexpected challenge to our thinking appears at the door when we are waiting for Sitt Wasfeyyah to arrive and teach our history class.

"*Walad!* A teenage boy!" Some girls gasp. "This is an all-girls school, and you should leave immediately," one girl shouts at the young man, who appears to be a couple of years older than us.

But he waves his hand to dismiss her, comes into our classroom, and stands in front of the chalkboard. He looks at our questioning faces and begins speaking. "I am a student in high school and care about my education, too. I am here to let you know that most of the students in Ramallah schools have taken to the streets today. A huge demonstration is forming." He uses hand gestures to emphasize his words. He urges us to leave school and join in the protest.

There is silence now.

"But did Um Nader, the principal of our school, permit you to come to our class and announce this news?" I ask.

"No," he replies with a tense smile. "I climbed over the barbed-wire fence in the backyard of the school."

I smile back because his answer reminds me of the time my older brothers and I climbed similar army fences near our stone house. The sense of triumph in being able to jump to the other side in spite of torn-up clothes and bleeding hands is unforgettable.

The young man then explains the urgent news about the Tal al-Zaatar refugee camp in Beirut, Lebanon. Created by UNRWA after the Nakba, it is less than one square mile and holds over fifty thousand Palestinian refugees. "The camp is under siege by armed Lebanese militias that want the Palestinians and the fedayeen out of Lebanon," he says. "The militias claim that there are fedayeen among the camp residents. Hundreds of people got killed, and the refugees inside are now starving and dying of thirst as we speak. We must all join the demonstration in the center of Ramallah," he urges. "We need to let our people in Lebanon know that they are not alone. And we need to chant loudly so that this world, which pretends deafness when it comes to our people, can hear us."

The young man waits, but none of us make a move to leave class. I do not know what to think, especially because I have never been to a demonstration, and Mother always warns against political involvement or doing anything with boys. I have heard that older students from high schools and colleges go to demonstrations often, and because demonstrations are about demanding our freedom, I am moved to join in though uncertain what to do.

The young man knocks on a desk three times, half begging, half commanding: "*Yallah, yallah*, come on! Stop being cowards!"

When we still don't speak or move a millimeter, he pulls out a piece of cloth from his pocket and unfurls it. "This is the Palestinian flag. We are not allowed to raise our flag anywhere because of the military occupation. But we will raise it no matter what during the demonstration. Let's go!"

I want to touch the outlawed flag, but I also worry that our school and especially our principal will be penalized if anyone finds out what is happening in our classroom. According to the military rules, we can go to prison for having a Palestinian flag or even drawing it. I have not seen a real cloth one before, although I have seen it drawn in graffiti on walls. But each time it is drawn differently, so I have never been certain until this moment how it really looks.

The young man bolts out of our class when Sitt Wasfeyyah comes. But now several other young men gather on the street outside the gate of our school and begin to throw stones at our school's playground and shout for everyone to join the demonstration. "Learn something about Palestine," one of them yells before he throws leaflets over the fence. Then the young men all disappear.

Um Nader comes and says we should go home. It is likely that clashes will happen, and perhaps a curfew will follow. "Take the shortest way," she instructs.

We begin packing our books to head out of school. I go to Sitt Wasfeyyah and ask her: "Why do you teach us geography and history about every country in Europe and Asia and nothing about Palestine?"

She stares at me with tears in her eyes, then puts her hand on my shoulder. "We do not choose the books or topics we teach and have strict regulations about what we can and cannot discuss in the classroom. If we teach about Palestine, we will be punished."

"Do you like to teach history?" I ask.

"Yes," she replies. "I like it more than any other subject I teach. With history one learns that nothing lasts. So it is only a matter of time before we will become free again. I do not know how long from now. But it will happen. Big change is the rule in history, not the exception."

"Do you dislike anything about history?"

"Yes. It also shows me that everyone loves freedom, but mostly for themselves and not for others. I read about the French and their great revolution, and then they went on to occupy so many nations and deprive them of freedom and rights. The Americans fought the occupation of the British but do not hold the same value for others."

I am learning things she never says in the classroom. She continues.

"Arabs also, we do not like to admit that our dominance over others was undesired by those who had to tolerate it. And the Ottomans, when they ruled over us, wanted to control the world. It seems that the idea of freedom for everyone everywhere is more hated than loved, resisted than encouraged. Talk of it is one thing, and refusing to grant or share equal freedom with others is behind most wars and difficult history."

I thank her and then, without hesitation, run in the direction of the demonstration to discover for myself what happens during one.

As I get closer to the city center I hear loud chanting. My heart pounds with the desire to be in the middle of the crowd. But I am only at the edge, moving slowly. Shopkeepers are standing on the sidewalks in front of their stores, ready to close up if there is trouble.

The older students who are demonstrating have covered their heads and faces with *kufiyyahs* so they won't be recognized. Someone is waving a large Palestinian flag back and forth. The flag is so big that I tremble as though all rules have been broken at once.

Listening to people speak around me, I learn more about what the boy mentioned in my classroom. A man says that if someone living in the Tal al-Zaatar camp goes out to get water from a well, even if it is after midnight, Lebanese militia snipers will kill him, hoping he will fall into the well and his blood will pollute the water. Bombs target the Palestinian refugee camps in Lebanon day and night. Outside the camps, people's dress codes, areas of residence, dialects, and ID cards, which specify their ethnic and religious affiliations, are all cause for instant assassination of those thought to be Palestinian.

"Why are the Lebanese doing this?" I ask the man. "Aren't they Arab like us?"

He explains that the political conditions in Lebanon are complicated, and not all the Lebanese are involved in the attacks against the camp. Some groups, like the militias called al-Kata'eb, the Phalangists, resent the many Palestinian refugees who went to Lebanon after the wars of 1948 and the Six-Day War in 1967. And then when the Palestinian fedayeen who escaped Jordan after Black September in 1970 went to Lebanon to fight Israel from the Lebanese border, it complicated the country's politics even more. But mainly, after we became refugees in other countries, we became easy targets for mistreatment. If we do nothing, the world ignores our plight. If we fight to regain our home, we cause problems. If we ask to be citizens in the countries where we are refugees, we are often rejected because these states do not want to grant us equal rights and and have us live with them forever.

The crowd starts to chant "Tal al-Zaatar" over and over again. Car tires are set on fire in protest. People in the crowd sing songs with a thousand emotions in their voices. I do not know the lyrics but catch a few lines, which I write in a notebook, hoping to learn the entire song later. Then army jeeps come. Israeli soldiers fire gunshots in the air. I rush home, thinking about the boy who came to our school and hoping that he is okay.

After that I begin to listen more closely to the news and the the hushed political conversations of the grownups and I try to understand what it means to be Palestinian. I gather that many groups of Palestinians are scattered in many, many places around the world. The word that describes our condition is *shatat*, diaspora.

I also begin to pay more attention to the graffiti on houses, shops, stone walls, and doors all over Ramallah, written with symbols and names and events and dates. These are references to shreds of our history as it was and as it unfolds. But it is hard to understand it. It is like a broken glass: endless small pieces that need to be put together.

At the end of the school year, I am no longer just focused on academic responsibilities. I am filled with bigger questions: Is being Palestinian bad? Would the world be happier if there were no Palestinians at all? I tell Ustaz Khaled my thoughts. He says that I must keep these matters out of my mind. The best triumph for a Palestinian is to finish school, he insists, and to stay alive, too, in order to do that. "Our lives are as important as anyone else's, as important as those of the prophets and scientists, army leaders, presidents of countries, and Adam and Eve in heaven. They are our parents. Yes?"

I nod, but I do not believe him. I do not feel that our lives are important to the world. What is important about a life without freedom?

Ustaz Khaled changes the subject and asks me what I plan to do during the summer.

"I want to work," I reply. He acts surprised, so I ask, "Should I not?"

"I am only wondering if your family will let you do it. But work is the best teacher," he says. "And I think that you can do anything you decide to do. So I will await a report from you when you return to school in September."

We wave goodbye and I run home determined to find a way to have a job, learn much, and surprise Ustaz Khaled.

Daring

"*Biddy ashtghel*, I want to work," I beg Mother. "You let Basel and Muhammad have a summer job selling ice cream, and you should let me have a summer job, too."

"How many times am I going to say no?" is her answer.

"Until you finally say yes, because I do not want to wear used clothes anymore."

A few times a year, we go to the UNRWA office to pick up a bundle of used clothes that people in other countries donate to the poor. When Mother opens it we are all hopeful for a near-new item that is our size.

Often we find things we can't wear, such as a dazzling blue party dress of sheer fabric that has a completely bare back. A girl in Ramallah cannot wear such a dress and walk near other girls covered in *hijab* and scarves without attracting everyone's ridicule. Once, I found a skirt adorned with rows of small beads, scarabs, and buttons that could have been donated by the queen of Palmyra from the third century. Washing it would have been impossible. Another time I found a pair of padded pants with zippers up to the knees. Later, I learned that they were ski pants. Had I worn them, everyone would have known that they weren't mine because no one skis in the West Bank.

Even so, the clothes are strange, pleasant, and surprising to look at, because they come from other countries and have the feel of other people's characters and lives in them. But they are also humiliating. I want outfits that I choose, that are completely mine from the first day they come from the shop until they fade and lose all their buttons.

The biggest present donated by people in other countries, however—and much better than clothes—is the Universal Declaration of Human Rights. I saw a summary of it posted on a wall at the UNRWA office. I read it and copied every word from it into my notebook. Later, I wrote the key words on a piece of paper I keep in my pocket.

I take it out often and think: All these thirty rights belong to me, too! What went wrong to have so many of them not present in my life? Having this paper encouraged me, so instead of saying *I have the right* to do something, I began saying *I have thirty rights* to do it. I read from the declaration to my mother and father and siblings, always personalizing it.

People of Ramallah are born free, that is article 1. All Palestinian refugees have the right to a nationality, that is article 15. My father has the right to rest, article 24. Everyone has the right to work, article 23. That is what I quote to Mother as we argue about my getting a job. I emphasize the word *everyone*.

"But what will people say about us?" she says. "The Barakats send a girl to work! What a scandal!"

But I know that the final decision will come from Father, so I go to him.

"*Yaba,*" I say. "Many nations in the world have agreed that I have the right to work. And it is written in this document." I point to the unfolded paper.

He raises his eyebrows.

Before he says anything, I tell him: "*Biddy ashtghel,* I want to find a summer job."

"Nothing that applies to other nations applies to us here under the occupation," he says. "Besides, it is *aayb,* socially wrong." He is annoyed by the very thought of a girl working.

Aayb is a reply I hear more than any other expression. This is the one word that can stand in the way of a girl like a roadblock. *Aayb* has thousands of years of people believing it, strengthening it. I don't think *aayb* should ever be said to someone wanting to work.

"Please let me work, even for a short time," I beg.

"You want men to laugh at me for not being able to support my family and protect my *sharaf,* my honor?"

Honor is the main reason something is described as socially wrong. Women in traditional Arab families represent the honor of the men in those families, and so many men, like my father, keep close watch over the actions of their female family members.

"But having a job *is* an honor," I protest. "Wasn't Khadeejah, the Prophet Muhammad's first wife, a businesswoman, and he was employed by her, too? That was many centuries ago. Do we move back in time or forward?"

"You are only twelve and a half years old. You do not know anything about the world."

"I want to begin now, and to know it from my own experience. You started working when you were eight."

"Khalas! The end!" He closes the conversation as if he were slamming a door.

I think about the dangerous word *honor.* I have heard stories of families who killed their daughters for what they called honor. When I hear this word, how I wish I were a boy. Not only would I be freer then, but I would argue and fight to help the girls in my family and in the world gain more freedom and more rights.

I do not argue with my parents about having a summer job again, but I begin to speak about my house chores as though they are paid work.

"Mother, I will do the dishes, and the compensation is that for one day, you do not criticize anyone or anything, especially me," I tell her.

"Only one hour, and only if I choose to," she bargains.

I decide to take the biggest risk I can imagine. One morning, when Basel and Muhammad wake up early to go sell the ice cream that they carry on their backs in thermoses, I get up with them. I wish I could sell ice cream, too. But I know the difference between daring and dangerous. Roaming the streets with my brothers would be dangerous for a girl my age.

Ten minutes after Father goes to work and my brothers leave, I tape a small note on the door for Mother: *Gone to find work*. I run out of the house to al-Manara, the center of Ramallah, and then to al-Sharea al-Ra'eesee, Main Street. The shops are not yet open, but there is a small group of women on one side of the street, and a group of men standing a short distance from them. I ask the women: "Is this where people wait for the bus to the industrial district?"

"Yes," a few reply.

"Which factory are you going to?"

"Tako, the paper tissue factory."

"Do you like working there?"

"We need the money."

"Nobody says bad things about your honor?"

"One cannot stop people from speaking, but we need to help feed our families."

I am now more at ease. The bus comes and in fifteen minutes we are at the entrance of Tako. Everyone punches a card to show their exact arrival time. I stand at the end of the line, and when I am the only one left, I ask the secretary who was supervising the workers checking in if I can have a job.

She says that I must wait. A man then comes and looks at me from head to toe. "How old are you?" he asks.

"Twelve and a half."

"You will be the youngest on the floor. Take a few days to do simple tasks and learn. Do what the supervisor says and avoid the big machines." As he walks away he turns around to add, "And no gossip. It distracts you and costs us money."

Inside the factory is an amazing world. Giant rolls of paper, the size of small cars and wider than bedsheets, are fixed on huge machines. There are hundreds of thousands of facial tissue boxes. An electric saw cuts cardboard. A conveyor belt moves pocket-size tissues like fish in a stream. Colorful boxes are stacked high. There is a whole wall of toilet paper rolls. The dust from cutting the paper looks like snow on some areas of the floor.

Abu Mousa, the supervisor, decides I should start at the station where tissue is tucked inside boxes. He points to a woman and says, "Work with her." Nahla is a tiny woman with a big smile. She appears to be in her twenties. Her complexion is purple dark, only a few shades lighter than night black. Her clothes are colorful, mixing red and orange and yellow like a basket of fresh fruit. "*Ahlan!* Welcome!" she says.

Nahla teaches me the proper way to fold a stack of facial tissue and put it inside a box. She warns about various machines, mentioning with extra seriousness that one factory worker damaged his hand by looking away for one second while cutting paper with a saw. "Don't let your mind wander while working with machines! If you can't help it, then stay at the folding and boxing tables." When Nahla is certain that I understand what I am supposed to do, she starts to gossip.

She mutters words under her breath while looking at her hands, so it doesn't look like she is speaking. But I can hear her clearly.

"That man, Qazem, over there with the thick hair like a short broom, and big muscles, avoid him! He follows girls and has a mean side although he pretends to be good when inside the factory. That thin boy with the light brown hair, Sergio, is the politest person you will ever meet." Sergio could not be much older than me, I think. "The older man carrying a mountain of boxes is a good man. He often works overtime to feed his many children."

Nahla comments on each person on the floor, including her sister, Laila, who is operating a machine and smiles from a distance as though she knows what Nahla is saying and doing.

"The secretary is always having a bad day and she thinks she is above us because her work is 'clean office work.' Can anyone say that our work is not clean? With all this tissue paper?" Nahla jokes cheerfully.

"The owners of the factory are three Armenian brothers. The man over there with the extremely curly hair is the big boss. His name is Vahan." I tell her he is the one who hired me. She nods. "He makes all the decisions. He never smiles, and one look from him is enough to make us double our production. When he's especially angry, he berates everyone for all kinds of reasons, including using too much toilet paper in the restroom."

I cover my face with my hands and giggle.

"That tall, good-looking man, he is the second brother. His

name is Serob, and he is the friendliest of the three. He speaks gently, says please and thank you, as though we are his friends, and does not shout at anyone. He plays the guitar. All the girls in the factory think he's attractive."

"My father is more handsome than he is," I say.

Nahla laughs and continues. "Then there is Levon, the third brother. He is extremely quiet and does the bookkeeping. If you ever hear him speak, you will qualify to win a prize."

After the half-hour lunch break, Nahla asks me about singers I like.

"Abdel Halim Hafez," I reply.

Like me, she knows many of his songs by heart. So we begin humming "Ahwak," or "I Love You."

We nod our heads and tap our feet gently to harmonize the pensive lyrics that paint the picture of a lover who tells his beloved that he wishes he could forget her, but not without forgetting his soul. If someday she forgot him, causing him to lose his soul, he would see that as an agreeable sacrifice for her love.

In the middle of the song she asks: "Do you like any boys?"

"I like the boy in *The Old Man and the Sea*, but he is imaginary."

"What?"

"He exists only on paper and in readers' minds. I can tell you the story sometime. And you?"

"I am having a difficult time getting married because my faith is Druze and there are not many Druze families in Ramallah. Besides, look at my skin, too dark for many men to find beautiful."

"You are beautiful," I tell her.

"I have a great life anyway." Nahla smiles, consoling herself. "And I believe in fate."

I ask about the Druze faith. She explains that in this religion you learn its core beliefs when you turn forty years old. That is when a person becomes responsible enough to decide to commit to it. She also explains that the Druze believe in the reincarnation of souls.

"What does that mean?" I ask.

Nahla speaks and I open my eyes wide as she describes reincarnation stories. One Druze woman Nahla mentions is fluent in many languages without ever having learned them. She had done so in a previous lifetime . . . A young girl sees an old man and announces that she was his mother. She knows his name and the names of everyone in his family and the games he liked to play when he was a child.

I am mesmerized and cannot get enough details. "You are certain that anyone can come back?"

"Yes," she assures me.

Nahla says that Farid al-Atrash, the famous Arab musician and singer, is Druze like she is. So we hum one of his songs about a lemon tree that knows the singer's suffering. I wonder if the lemon tree could have been another tree, pomegranate or pear, in a previous lifetime, too, and been reincarnated.

At the end of the day, I clock out and ride the bus to the center of Ramallah, then run home. I stand for a few minutes before entering the house because I have no idea what to expect.

Upon seeing me, Mother slaps me across the face. Many hours pass before the prints of her fingers leave my cheek. But I argue with her: "You work all day at home and you do not get paid. I am not going to have the same life as yours."

The next day, I do the same: run away in the morning and come back in the late afternoon. Father says that they will have to lock me up in the house. But I escape again and go to the factory. I hear more stories from Nahla. I dream of reincarnating as a free person.

Suddenly my parents give up trying to make me stay at home and surprise me by agreeing that I can work. "As long as you stay away from boys and men," they insist.

"I promise."

We get paid at the end of the week, and I buy some of the family necessities and put them on the table with a note written in large letters: *For my father: Only now am I beginning to know what you feel when you work for pay, and how much it takes for you to feed and support a family of nine people.* I also tell him that he is handsomer than Serob, the co-owner of Tako. Father smiles as he slowly reads the note. He then repeats out loud what I wrote to Mother.

My days begin to have a rhythm: waking up early with the birds, going to the factory, listening to gossip and the hum of machines, watching trucks come to take full boxes of tissue to city stores, seeing machines break down, a worker almost getting cut by belts breaking suddenly, and having a lot of time to hum songs and think. I realize that what the workers say about our low wages is right, and I understand their whispers about the need to form a workers' union. But for me, the payment I get is much more than the cash.

One week when we are standing in line to get our wages, everyone is cheerful, anticipating the weekend. We are chattering, including the older man, whom Nahla mentioned has many children and works overtime to feed them. He is speaking louder than all of us. Once in a while, this man helps me when he sees me struggling to carry a big box. He calls me *ya binti*, my daughter.

The secretary appears in her office, holding everyone's pay. She sits behind a glass panel that separates us from her. We receive our cash payments through an arched mouse-hole-size opening in the lower part of the panel. She asks that we stop talking and stand in a straight line.

The old man does not stop speaking right away. Impatient, she insults him. Dangling the money from her hand, she orders that he stand in line quietly. Her eyes become big like an owl's and her cheeks are red in anger. He complies.

Never before did I think I would ever feel the fury I am now feeling as the old man stands looking at the ground in shame. She spoke to him in a degrading way, violating article 5 of the Declaration of Human Rights.

I watch the secretary and the man. When it is his turn, she gives him his money slowly, making him keep his hand open longer than the other workers.

When he leaves and it is my turn, I ask the secretary for an apology to the man and all of us. "We are here to work, not be humiliated. We get enough humiliation from living under harsh military rule."

She stares at me in disbelief. Everyone in the line is so quiet that the traffic outside on the road is suddenly audible. The tension, if increased one more bit, might shatter the glass wall between us.

She puts my pay in front of me. "Take it," she grunts.

"Not until you apologize to this man and to all of us." I stare back at her.

Vahan appears in the room behind the secretary to ask what is going on. She turns her back to us and speaks to him in a low voice. When she faces the workers again she says, "I will *not* apologize to anyone!"

I am hoping that Vahan will say something to her or to us. He does not. He also does not ask any of us to explain our side of what happened.

Looking at me, then at all of the workers, he has no expression on his face, and he quickly disappears. So I announce, "I quit!" I leave my pay behind, and walk out of the factory alone. I wonder what my teacher Ustaz Khaled would say if he saw what just happened.

I do not tell my parents about quitting the job. I continue to go out early every day, looking for new work. After a week I have found nothing. So I go to the public library every day to write letters to my pen pals to see what they are doing during their summer vacations. I also discover many books I have never heard of. One day I open the English-Arabic dictionary randomly to a page and take the first word I see, *start*, to be a key word about my future. *Start* whispers to me to never hold back when one action ends and a new one must be taken.

A driver from the Tako factory comes to my home and brings me my pay, saying that everyone wants me to come back, the owners and the workers. But he mentions nothing about the secretary and the old man. So I decide that by going back and acting as though earning a wage is more important than my dignity, every moment at the factory would be unbearable for me. I would be violating my own rights. I still want to find another job. But suddenly life at home changes in ways that make being home as exciting as going to work. The world comes to us instead of us going to the world.

Chocolate

Mother has convinced Father to buy a black-and-white television set and make payments over a year. Our lives change from the first minute the TV is delivered to the small table covered with a special embroidered cloth in the corner of the room prepared for it. Another knit cloth sits on the side for covering the screen and protecting it from dust when it's not in use.

The delivery man explains there are two channels broadcast from Jordan: channel two, in Arabic, and channel six, in English. There are four hours of Arabic programming every evening, but on Friday there are special shows during the day. There is also an Israeli channel in Hebrew that airs a nightly newscast in Arabic and a weekly Arabic sitcom.

We gather on the floor around the TV to watch the Arabic channel. At six p.m., the entertainment begins, with many

Disney cartoons. Woody Woodpecker sounds like a wonderful typewriter that I wish I could have. Next are *Popeye*, *Abbott and Costello*, *Scooby-Doo*, and finally *Mickey Mouse*. The cartoons are subtitled in Arabic, but I do not look because I want to learn more English.

At first my younger brothers, Jamal, now almost three; Najm, four; and Samer, six, are quiet while watching cartoons, mesmerized by the movement on the screen. Then they begin to shout and interact with all the characters. The first time one of their heroes is hit so hard that stars circle around his head, they worry he will die and they rush behind the television to rescue him.

When they do not find him, they say, "Where are youuu!" mimicking Scooby-Doo. We are all relieved to realize that cartoon characters do not ever die.

Soap operas follow the cartoons. They are mostly love stories about men and women who are attracted to each other but do not confess it. There is jealousy, fear, lying, detective work, dreaming, sadness, loss, revenge, and theft, as well as conflict between rich families and poor families when love crosses over economic class norms. The best soap operas are based on novels by famous Egyptian authors such as Ihsan Abdel Quddous and Naguib Mahfouz.

The nightly news airs last. It is an hour, with half of it for regular news and the other half for sports. There is not one night when we do not see the king and queen of Jordan in the first half of the broadcast.

My older brothers wait impatiently to see if the sports seg-
ment will report on international and Jordanian soccer games.
The Palestinian refugee camps in Jordan have strong soccer
teams and we cheer for them. My brothers also learn about
the international soccer games that are replayed in their en-
tirety on the Jordanian television on Friday.

We watch the Israeli news channel to hear about the West
Bank and Gaza—mainly curfews, strikes, demonstrations, political developments, and military operations, in addition to
the weather. Neither the Jordanian nor the Israeli television
stations report on day-to-day Palestinian news. I wish we had
even one Palestinian radio station or a Palestinian television
channel.

On Friday evenings, the Jordanian television airs the most
anticipated event of the week, a two-hour Egyptian movie,
when the most famous actors and actresses entertain us as
we eat dinner. So we learn more of the Egyptian dialect and
use the strange fun words to make jokes and to imitate the
actors. We also learn that in movies there are scenes of seduc-
tive belly dancing and scenes of passionate kissing between a
man and a woman. The soap operas never show that.

When the belly dancer appears, my parents say harsh words
describing her as a fallen woman, but they go on watching her
every move. They also tell Mona and me to look away anytime
a kiss is about to happen. My brothers, because they are boys,
can continue to watch. I want to take out the human rights

declaration and plaster it on the television screen so they see nothing but how their discrimination is wrong.

At first, to avoid creating a problem, I turn my face away as instructed. I then begin to sit behind everyone. This way, if my parents turn to make sure that I am not looking, they will also have to miss the kissing scene. Restricting my freedom will cost them theirs for that moment.

On television, I also learn for the first time what Abdel Halim Hafez, the famous Egyptian love singer, looks like during his performances. He has an exceptionally big smile and piercing onyx eyes. His feelings well up from the depths of every sound he makes as he sings about love.

When we watch Nadia Comăneci receive perfect scores in gymnastics and win gold medals at the Montreal Olympics, Mona and I celebrate in Ramallah because even though Nadia is Romanian, she is brown-haired and looks Arab. Many girls in Ramallah are named Nadia. And like us she lives in hard political conditions imposed on her country by the Russian authorities. But Nadia wins a place in history in spite of that. Mona and I also marvel that she, like all the other gymnasts with her, appears on the screen dressed in a bathing suit in front of a large crowd. Mona nudges me and whispers: "Look! People are not angry to see a girl wearing a bathing suit in public. She is doing the splits, and everyone is cheering her agility and power. Can you believe Mother won't let us ride a bicycle?"

On the inside of our closet, Mona and I have taped pictures

of girls and women we admire. We add Nadia's picture to remind us it is good for a girl to be daring. We put her next to a drawing of my favorite scientist, Marie Curie, and a drawing of Mona's hero, Florence Nightingale.

I am now feeling even more confident than before that I have the right to be daring. I still want to work again before the new school year begins. So I go to Ramallah's industrial district to apply for a job at the Silvana chocolate factory.

As I walk toward the factory, I realize that the entire building is enveloped in a thick, warm chocolate aroma. It extends to the street and over the fields, infusing the air over the other factories with a festive smell.

"Hired!" a manager says after I mention that I have previous factory experience. He does not ask why I left. He takes me inside and I can hardly believe my eyes. Everywhere I turn there is chocolate candy: extremely big bars that get cut up into smaller pieces, stacks of chocolate-filled wafers, rows of lollipops, moving conveyor belts with small pieces of foil-wrapped chocolate rushing like miniature cars, then getting dumped into a box with a pink drawing of an eagle soaring over mountains. The wrappers are gold, silver, red, yellow, and green.

"Pick a station," the manager says. "It does not matter which." I choose the conveyor belt carrying already wrapped pieces. My job there, he explains, is to make certain that all the pieces stay on the belt and to throw any incompletely wrapped piece into a bucket on the side. After an hour of checking every piece, I ask the woman working a few yards away from me if it is all right to taste the chocolate.

She smiles and says a cook of anything, even poison, cannot help tasting it. But not while working; eating is during lunchtime only.

"How many pieces can I have?" I ask.

"As much as you desire, one piece or a hundred," she says, laughing. "Try everything. But you cannot take any of it home. That is the rule. Workers who do that will be fired. Nothing inside pockets, purses, or under a hat. You must buy what you want to take home."

"What about the wrappers? I would like to wrap my books with them if I can."

"Collect them from the pieces you eat. Perhaps you can tape them on the book covers?" she suggests.

At lunchtime I sit with pieces of every kind of candy made in the factory next to me in a brown bag. I cross my legs on the thin wooden bench in the hot sun, and in half an hour I have a little pile of empty wrappers next to me. I smooth them flat and stack them inside my notebook to take home.

My co-workers say they did the same when they first started, but they quickly learned that chocolate increases acne because of the fat in it, and creates problems with teeth because of the sugar. Chocolate, many warn me, also has the same effect as coffee on sleep.

After work, I buy a box of chocolates to take home. It contains fifty small pieces. I gather my younger brothers and have them close their eyes. I pour the box over their heads like rain. When they open their eyes they pretend that the chocolates are fish and they are swimming among them, catching one and eating it every few minutes.

Within a week, I discover that my co-workers were right in the advice they gave. I have a difficult time falling asleep, so I call it the choco-late factor. With one last piece of chocolate I could not bear to eat, I write on a big rock outside our house, using the chocolate like chalk. Ants appear from everywhere and fill the outlines of the letters.

"What's that?" Mona asks.

"Chocol-ant, a new type font that combines chocolate and ants," I say.

After two weeks at Silvana, I wish that the sweet smell was not there. Whenever I see chocolate I have no desire to touch it.

And then all things seem to lose their sweetness after I hear the news that the Tal al-Zaatar Camp in Lebanon fell. The surrendering of the camp led to a massacre of thousands of Palestinian refugees. Because we are not supposed to discuss politics at the factory, I battle my sadness alone while working.

On the last day of summer vacation, I say goodbye to Silvana and prepare for school. I buy a new pair of shoes, a jacket, a schoolbag, and the books I need. I decide that I will never wear donated clothes again even if I have to wear these clothes I have just bought forever. All my books are covered with glittering thin wrappers, and I am excited about seeing Ustaz Khaled again.

"What five things did you learn this summer?" he asks.

"How to fold tissue paper. The Druze faith teaches about reincarnation. Speak up for someone else and seek justice even if it is not there. A girl can become a world champion in a way no one else has done before. And chocolate keeps you up at night.

"I also have a sixth thing," I add. "I memorized the spelling of hundreds of new English words. I used the dictionary and cartoons on TV as my English tutors."

"I will quiz you on them all," he says, smiling. After that, whenever Ustaz Khaled sees me, he asks for the spelling and meaning of two or three difficult English words.

Contest

After the first month of eighth grade, there is an announcement at school about an English composition contest the UNRWA educational office will hold for all the United Nations–run refugee middle schools in the West Bank and Gaza. On the basis of our grades, my classmates Dawlat and Najwa and I qualify as candidates.

A committee is formed to evaluate the three of us and decide who will represent the school. Dawlat and I remain in the final round. "The contest will be held in the middle of December. Are you willing to work as hard as possible in the next two and a half months?" we are asked. We both say yes. All teachers at the school are invited to give their opinions about who is more likely to win.

My Arabic creative writing teacher volunteers that I am the only student she has who disputes her grades. She always gives me 23 out of 25, and I always ask her where I made a mistake that justifies subtracting two points. She never underlines anything or makes notes in the margins of my papers.

She replies that no one gets a perfect score in creative writing.

"Why?" I ask.

Laughing, she says that not even Taha Hussein, the famous Egyptian author known as the dean of Arabic literature, can get a perfect score. She explains that in creative arts, perfection can never be reached and there is always room to do better.

"What you are saying does not help me learn," I protest, looking at the ground to hide my tears.

But her comment weighs in my favor even though the upcoming contest is going to be in English, not Arabic. So when the evaluation is completed, the committee determines that I will represent my school. Ustaz Khaled says this is just one step in a long journey. I must begin the work immediately.

Because this is the first contest, there is no previous winner to learn from. If there were, I would search for the address of that student's school and mail a pen pal invitation for him or her to correspond with me.

To prepare, I must spend an hour every day after school with Sitt Afaf, an English teacher who discusses English comprehension with me, listens as I read passages from stories, and has me put English words into sentences. Accuracy is essential. And I have to speak about everything in English.

"Make the mistakes now," she encourages. "That way I can

teach you something you need. Good learners are the ones who make mistakes and correct them."

"Why does the word *believe* have *lie* at its center?" I ask. "Should a person believe a lie?"

She looks at the word and at me. "A good question," she praises. "Now you will remember how to spell *believe* by the word *lie*, which must not be believed."

When Sitt Afaf is satisfied that I have made progress for the day, Ustaz Khaled takes over, asking me to build English sentences in the past, past perfect, and conditional future tenses. He introduces adjectives, adverbs, commas, semicolons, and periods. When I am tired, I say, "Could the present tense relax? It is too tense." He smiles and I have a break.

"You see words in a different way," he comments. "What do they mean to you?"

"Everything," I reply. "The word *spell* does not only mean to list the letters but to cast a magic spell by saying the right words. If the reader is not affected, then the spelling is wrong even if the letters are all in the correct place."

"I think that we are sending a poet to the contest," he says, laughing. "Poetry is the gift of Arabs, even if you are preparing for a contest in English."

As the weeks pass and it gets closer to December, when I will participate in the contest, I am ready to prove my teachers right in their confidence in me. At home, I spend every minute writing about what happened during my day as though I am being tested. Because I've been focusing on one project for so long, many things around me change without my noticing, including my sister, Mona, who used to ask me daily for help with her math homework. She always confuses the numbers 2 and 6, as they are the mirror image of each other in Arabic. Now she has begun to complete her assignments by herself.

The night before the contest I push my papers aside and ask Mona how she is doing in math. She shows me a recent test with a perfect score on it, in spite of her continuing to confuse 2 and 6. As I read her solutions, I see that she has solved each problem containing either 2 or 6 twice, the first time as though the indicated number is a 2 and the second as though it is a 6. The teacher rewarded her honesty and cleverness. I embrace Mona and feel that she has an approach to solving problems that is entirely her own.

In the morning, Mother chases me with an egg sandwich and a cup of milk. "They said on the radio protein is necessary for good thinking."

I arrive at school early; all the teachers are waiting for me. They ask if I have everything I need. I tell them I do, and Ustaz Khaled asks, "Tell us now, why are you going to win?"

I reply that in addition to loving to write with all my heart, I want to honor the efforts of my teachers and the name of my school. Then I add that this is also the first time I am competing with boys, not just with girls from all-girl schools. So this is my chance to show myself and the boys and girls of all the UNRWA middle schools what a girl from Ramallah can do.

My teachers are happy with my confidence. Sitt Afaf arranges my school uniform's white collar around my neck and gives me her comb to take with me. "You will do much better if you look neat," she says. She then gives me directions to the competition site, which is an hour's walk from my school, at al-Amari refugee camp school, which has a large auditorium that can hold many contestants. "Leave now so that you will be there earlier than the other contestants," Sitt Afaf says.

As my schoolmates enter classes for the first period, I walk out of the gate toward al-Amari camp. Everyone on the playground waves to encourage me. I warm up my mind by describing everything I see in complete sentences, as though I am a radio announcer.

When I arrive, the proctors are waiting. One of them asks me to choose a seat. I pick the desk closest to the door as I always do, thinking that it will be easy to escape if something bad happens.

I examine every detail in the auditorium: the seats are far away from each other, and everything is organized for the competition, contrary to the disorganized camp scene outside the school with thousands of tin-roofed shacks squished together.

At the front of the room stacks of notebooks and boxes of yellow pencils are ready on a table. A white screen covers the entire blackboard. In half an hour, the room fills with the contestants, each taking a desk. Then a bell rings announcing it's ten a.m., the time to distribute the test notebooks and pencils.

We must not open our notebooks or touch our pencils until instructed.

I gaze at my yellow pencil. It reminds me of a prize I received as a first grader, a yellow pencil and a rubber ball. A teacher said then: *The pencil to write with. The ball to see what resilient means: to bounce back higher.*

Finally, a proctor reveals the competition assignment: "Look at the white screen covering the chalkboard. Write about what you see. You have five minutes for questions. After that no speaking is allowed."

I stare at the screen. I had been thinking from the minute I arrived that the essay topic must be hidden on the blackboard underneath the screen. But there is no topic, nothing at all.

"I do not see anything on the screen," one contestant in the back complains. "I need to move closer to the front." A second voice and then a third say the same thing. They are almost crying and their voices are shaking. But I am right in front of the screen and, like them, I see nothing. So I, too, am perplexed.

The proctor tells them that there is nothing written on the screen and that it is time for us to open our notebooks and begin writing.

I decide that if nothing is on the screen, then the assignment is about what is not visible. That seems strange since no one has ever asked such a question at school. But this is a contest and can have new things, just like tests have new questions. I remember Ustaz Khaled saying he was sure only one person could answer the riddle about the coin, and I hear him in my mind now, saying, *I am sure only one person can see what is on the board.* So I begin writing:

Here on this white screen, there used to be a country made of many cities that you can count as you ride the bus. Many families lived there, but something happened and all of them lost their ability to count. They began to feel blank. They kept losing, and it was like an eraser was following them wherever they walked, erasing their steps until all that remains is this blank board.

In this blank city in front of me, there is a girl, and this board is how she feels, blank. She has many friends who feel the same blank way. One day, today, she and her friends agree to change things. So when food is needed in the city, they draw food colors on this board. But they are worried about running out of color and being left with only the screen.

They are thinking: If we raise the screen, under it we will find the blackboard and inside the board there is the night. In the night, buried, are the sadness and the dead colors of the sunrise from fights between the light of summer and the darkness of winter. If we bury the dead colors, they will feed the earth and make it grow flowers that will bring butterflies and wake up the feeling of happiness in everyone in the lost country. The blank becomes a blanket that we can sit on by the sea in one of the seasons and see everything.

This screen is not a screen. It is a scream. I hear it loud

as a cloud in winter that becomes a thundercloud. I hear its
blank loud enough to write what it tells me made it blank,
made it look like an eye without even one blink. I cry for it,
and ink drops fall on my paper like tears.

Finished writing, I give my notebook to the proctor. "You have half an hour left. I think you should revise!" she says. But I leave without changing a word.

"How was the contest?" my teachers ask. I tell them the details. They find it strange and wonder how other students responded to the challenge. Everyone must wait until the contest results are announced on March 31.

I forget about that date as the first half of the school year is completed, and I join everyone in Ramallah in thinking about the news, which is now filled with reports, analysis, and predictions about the United States with its new president, Jimmy Carter. Because the United States supports Israel, many Palestinians believe that ending the Israeli occupation can be achieved only if a US president and the US Congress want it. Politics and hopes of freedom dominate my mind until spring comes.

On March 31, Ustaz Khaled stands in front of everyone gathered on the playground after recess and announces that the UNRWA educational office has released the name of the winner of the writing contest. He does not look at me or even in my direction. I am overwhelmed with the desire to know who won. But he changes the subject, talking about how girls need to be powerful and creative, while all the female teachers stand quietly behind him. Only Sitt Afaf is not there.

Ustaz Khaled even finds a way to link his talk to the death of Abdel Halim Hafez, the singer of love songs who died this week at age forty-seven. Millions of people walked in his funeral in Egypt. The news announced that some girls committed suicide when hearing of his passing. I held his picture and wept as though he were a relative of mine.

"Like you, I love singers," Ustaz Khaled says. "But to kill oneself because a singer died? What about the songs in you? We want and need people who love and give their hearts to the world, like Abdel Halim himself did."

I have a hard time focusing on his words and am thinking that unless our school has won, there would be no need to announce anything. Is he going to announce that we lost? Maybe all schools are required to make the announcement. Ustaz Khaled continues speaking about many topics that he seems to have saved up for this day.

Then suddenly, he says, "It is my great pleasure to announce that our school has won first place in the first West Bank and Gaza UNRWA contest for English composition. And the winner is ... Samia!"

I look at Samia and she looks at me. Her English is good because she went to a private English-speaking school before coming here. But she did not compete. "Oh, an early April Fools', everyone," Ustaz Khaled says.

He is playing as usual. Then he corrects himself: "The winner is Ibtisam." He says it as though he has not spent dozens of hours teaching me and teasing me as he tested my knowledge.

He raises his arm and points to where we see Sitt Afaf walking out of the main school building carrying a huge box. She hands it to Ustaz Khaled, who, with great delight, proceeds to open it and place its contents on a table prepared for this purpose.

After he finishes taking all the things out of the box, he raises each item and shows it to everyone on the playground: colorful paper, scissors that cut zigzags, glue bottles, books, an English dictionary, notebooks, study cards, an address book, stickers, erasers, and pens and crayons that are all shiny and beautiful, sent from another country. Not even one word of Arabic is inside the box.

When done, Ustaz Khaled puts everything back in the box and calls me to where the teachers gather to shake my hand, all of them saying: "*Mabrook!* Congratulations, our Ibtisam!" I look at their smiling eyes.

"Today, other schools are envious of us," Ustaz Khaled says.

"Including boys' schools?" I ask.

"Including boys' schools," he says, laughing.

Everyone applauds.

At home, Mother goes through the box the minute I arrive,

just like Ustaz Khaled did. She is so happy it is as if she has won it herself. Then she stares at me for a minute, her eyes saying something I have not seen in them before.

"The time has come," she begins. "I want to speak to you about something only you can help me with."

I listen eagerly.

Agreement

"You know that I left school after the sixth grade, got engaged when I was fourteen, and married at fifteen," Mother says. Hearing this I dart an impatient look at the ceiling because I am already bored. She has mentioned this fact more times than I have heard mosque prayers and church bells in Ramallah. She ignores my look and continues: "How would you feel if you were made to leave school this year?"

"I am horrified by the thought," I say. "It would be worse than death."

"That is how I felt, and I continue to feel this terrible pain every day. You can help me change that and have a new life!"

"Me?"

She nods.

"How?"

"I have a plan. And it is extremely simple." She lowers her

voice to make it sound not only simple but simpler than a whisper. "If you teach me everything you learn in your classes—everything—down to the smallest note, then I will learn the entire curriculum."

"Teach you everything?" I am hardly able to imagine what that means. "But then how will you get a formal certificate?"

"Now that you ask," she says, smiling broadly, "al-Urduneyyah, the Jordanian Secondary School. It's a private high school in al-Bireh that offers classes starting with the tenth grade, and nontraditional students can study in class or at home. I need you to help me bridge the distance from where I left off through the end of ninth grade. Then I can enroll in high school classes at al-Urduneyyah. If I pass the supervised exams of the tenth, eleventh, and twelfth grades, then I can sit for the comprehensive Tawjihi exams and get my high school diploma."

I am following Mother's every word, realizing how ambitious her plan is. Al-Bireh is the twin city of Ramallah, and to walk there from where we live in Ein Musbah would take an hour each way. And Mother left school over twenty years ago and now has seven children. For her to accomplish what she is describing will require so much effort. Whether or not she can do it, we will only discover over time. We do not know any women in our family, or in the many neighborhoods where we have lived, who have done this.

"I will be the first married woman with children in our family to go to high school," she says.

Being first to do something is one of Mother's special pleasures in life. The Presto pressure cooker sitting in our kitchen is one example. When it first appeared on the market, most of her friends and relatives did not buy it because they worried it might explode and harm them. But Mother said she had to have one. "Nobody who is afraid to take a risk can accomplish anything," she said. When she cooked the first meal in it she ordered all of us to stay outside the house just in case something went wrong. We watched her cook through the window. The meal was ready in thirty minutes instead of the usual two hours.

"What do you say?" She taps my shoulder. "Ready for the adventure?"

I am thinking about how this can be accomplished, imagining running home from school to begin another shift, skipping all extracurricular activities. On some days, like all mothers, she will be mad at something for reasons I do not understand. She could also refuse to do homework and I would not be able to do anything about it. I would not be able to throw chalk from the back of the room, like Ustaz Khaled does in my classroom, and then say: *Mom, your brain, use it or lose it.* I am thinking and I don't know what to say, wondering if I am being asked to carry a mountain.

She rushes to convince me. "From day to day it will become easier," she says. "I will study hard."

Suddenly, she does not need to explain any further. My decision is made. I am committed to teaching her as much as I am committed to my own studies. "Mother, I will help you achieve your dream in every way I can."

"May Allah bless you the number of stars at night and the number of words in books," she says.

Starting my new job without delay, I tell her that she can begin studying this year's notes, and as we discover gaps in her knowledge, we can review and study materials from previous years. She agrees.

I pull out a notebook that I do not need for the next day and hand it to her. "Begin with history," I instruct. "Here are all the notes. Stay away from the World Wars for a while, and especially the Sykes-Picot agreement, in which England and France divided the Middle East between them. That will make you angry and perhaps not want to read more.

"Review the pages about the Abbasid era, when Arabs enjoyed a glorious civilization and had the mind-set you have now. They saw no limits! Or read anything you like, because if you are inspired by a story you will remember it. You may like stories about Saladin and the liberation of Jerusalem from the Crusaders around nine hundred years ago."

The following week, curious about al-Urduneyyah school, I ask at the public library and discover that it is mainly for Palestinian men who were imprisoned for political reasons and then released, those who must work and study at the same time, or those with difficult circumstances that prevent them from being in regular schools requiring daily attendance. The women students at al-Urduneyyah are so few they could be counted at a glance.

But mainly I wonder what Father will do when Mother goes to study with men, contrary to the common social norms that prefer separation between boys and girls and men and women. When I ask Mother about this, she says not to mention al-Urduneyyah to Father. "For now we can say that I plan to go back to school without specifying which one. When it is time to tell him about al-Urduneyyah, Allah will help me find the right words to explain that a co-ed school is my only available option." I agree with her that now nothing matters other than bringing her to the level of the materials I am studying.

As I teach her I begin to see that she learns faster than I had expected, and she responds with unbending determination, making her dream part of everything she does: while cooking, cutting up the onions and frying them, as they sizzle in the pan, she reads a passage. She adds salt to the soup and names the longest river in the world. She goes outside to hang a shirt on the clothesline and says the equation "Speed equals distance divided by time." She increases her speed and shortens the distance and time between her current situation and her dream. She sweeps the floor and imagines that the tile squares are countries. She lists ten countries in Europe and their capital cities. When she sees a boot she says, "This is the map of Italy." She cleans the windows and spells a word in English. Her books have oil smudges, water and soup stains, and little sprinkles of spices. She uses a dried orange peel as a bookmark.

She covers the walls of her and Father's bedroom with pieces of paper big and small, all hanging from Scotch tape. That saves her the few minutes she would need to find something she has written down in a notebook. Her eyes are always going to one spot on the wall or another as she memorizes. When she's done with one subject, she changes the papers.

Father gazes at all the notes. Sometimes he becomes curious about a word or two and asks me to explain their meanings, which I try to do by simplifying the concepts and making them relevant to his own experiences.

At night, she has a book under her pillow and a book in her handbag, which rests on the bed next to her. A third one is open between her hands. She reads it in the bright light of a lamp and adjusts her body from side to side when her muscles are cramped from being in the same position. She sleeps on hard questions so that she can think through them in dream time. Father's snoring no longer bothers her.

The neighbors see Mother studying all the time. She tells them she has a dream and is working on it. They raise their eyebrows and say nothing. She prefers to think it is the silence of admiration.

Girls at my school hear about Mother studying the same subjects we are and ask me with a giggle: "Is it true? Is your mother in the same grade we are?"

"Yes," I reply. "What grades are your parents in?"

They giggle more.

During the three months of the summer vacation after

eighth grade, I tutor Mother intensively. I create quizzes and tests for her, and she completes the eighth-grade curriculum with ease, proving better at history, geography, and Arabic than some of my classmates. Her smile is so big she looks like a different woman. "Go have a photo made of you smiling this way," I tell her. "We have a new person in the house, and she is the student you."

But she disagrees. "Only when I get my Tawjihi certificate will the day be worth remembering."

When I begin ninth grade, continuing to tutor Mother month after month, not even the shocking visit of Egyptian president Anwar Sadat to Jerusalem makes Mother and me change our focus. While the West Bank is put under curfew to prevent any street protests during his visit—leaving everyone in Ramallah to lament that President Sadat broke the previous Egyptian commitment to help the Palestinians gain freedom from Israeli occupation—Mother says that education is the only real hope for Palestinian independence.

But then our relatives in Jerusalem learn about Mother's plans and come to visit us to voice their opinions. A few say they are proud of her. Grandma Fatima comes, too. Her basket is filled with plump purple grapes. She tells us that Aunt Amina in Jordan now has two sons in addition to her eleven daughters. But all Mother wants to talk about is education. Grandma says that Mother cannot be stopped. She encourages Mother by telling her that she would have done the same if she had had the chance. Father nods his head in wistful agreement.

But other relatives disagree. "You have seven children. It is *aayb*, shameful," they admonish. To Father they say, "How can you let her do this?" and warn him of the consequences.

They say the problem is that women should not do certain things and that they must honor the traditional social expectations.

Father replies that it makes no difference to him if Mother reads novels she likes or reads schoolbooks. Because Mother studies at home, he does not see a problem with her actions. Father does not say that he and Mother have had fewer fights since she began studying and that he enjoys the new peace her studying offers their relationship. But I know that.

As I listen I see that Mother is a mix of extreme upholding of traditions and extreme rebellion against traditions. I am certain that no one else has a mother like mine.

She argues with our relatives, defending a woman's right to work, to speak, to say no, to do anything she needs to be strong and independent. I do not remind her of how she resisted my working earlier. She does not like anyone to point out her inconsistencies.

I am glad that Mother has changed. The more I learn, the more I change, too, I tell myself. She is also growing. Studying helps expand the mind by offering new perspectives and the bigger picture. By changing our own lives, Mother, Mona, and I are struggling to change what a girl can do.

But in the spring of ninth grade, the entire West Bank is astonished by news of the actions of a twenty-year-old

Palestinian woman, Dalal al-Mughrabi. In comparison, Mother trying to go back to school, Mona finally knowing how to distinguish between the numbers 2 and 6, me working, or even all of us climbing Mount Everest—if we were ever to do so—feels like nothing more than boiling an egg in the kitchen.

Dalal, a young woman from a Palestinian refugee camp in Lebanon and a member of the Palestine Liberation Organization, infiltrated the Israeli border, leading a group of armed fedayeen. She and her group hijacked an Israeli bus to avenge the killing of a Palestinian military leader.

There was more than thirty hours of shooting and fierce fighting, with blood in the streets, sirens everywhere, many people injured, and others killed, including Dalal. Everyone in Ramallah is shocked that a young woman would do all this.

The girls in my school are moved to tears by Dalal's story. They whisper that if we had a country and an army, she would be one of the heroes, like the men who carry arms and fight and die for their people's freedom. We would name a street after her. Had she lived, she might have become the head of the country, like Menachem Begin, the current Israeli prime minister, who once led a group that committed many massacres in the struggle to create the nation of Israel.

Some of the girls want to name their future daughters Dalal. But it is not the name that shapes a person, I think, for I have an aunt named Dalal. My aunt cannot even get her husband to stop smoking in their bedroom.

Dalal's name, however, on Palestinian tongues, begins to

mean courage and resistance rather than its dictionary meaning, which is flirtation. The Israeli newscasters, while mourning their dead, describe Dalal and her group as the most
dangerous of terrorists. Israeli military leaders promise severe
retaliation against the Palestinians.

I ask myself what I would say to the world if I published a
newspaper. The thought fills me with possibilities. So I bring
home a newspaper and cut out articles, words, pictures, head-
lines, ads, different fonts, and numbers.

I decide to put the words in different places. Now the word
Palestinian is in the place of the word *Israeli*, and *Israeli* in the
place of *Palestinian*. What a new world! *Menachem Begin*, the
name of the Israeli prime minister, is switched with *Dalal
al-Mughrabi*, and now he is the terrorist. *Dalal al-Mughrabi* is in
another column about fashion, hair rollers, and beauty.

I write an article in which she is being interviewed by angels and she says that she did not want to die or to kill anyone,
but all the sorrow she saw in her twenty years of life as a
Palestinian refugee made death better than life for her.

Then I put the words *violence, retaliation*, and *terrorism* in the
obituaries section. Among the dead I place military occupa-
tions from anywhere in the world. Among the dead I place all
weapons. Among the dead I place cruelty. Among the dead I
place discrimination. Among the dead I place history that repeats itself.

I write a commentary under the headline "The War of the
Cousins." *Awlad ammna*, our cousins, is the name we call Jews

because we come from the same father, Abraham. Their mother is Sarah; ours is Hagar. The article shows how all the violence among people is family violence.

In an interview with Alfred Nobel, who invented dynamite, I spell *dynamite* in the headline as *die-na-might*, and he asks forgiveness for the damage his invention has caused many people.

There is no editor to fight with me about the news. No censor. So I continue. Among the birth announcements, I place freedom for everyone, and a hospital for everyone's visible and invisible wounds. Whole nations can be admitted free of charge to this hospital so that they can recover from harsh histories.

Now I publish my newspaper. I realize the pair of scissors and bottles of glue I got from the contest are real presents. The paper looks like it has gone through an operation and is healing, all of its wounds closing. I call it a *muse paper* and continue creating muse papers, changing painful articles about Northern Ireland, Cuba, Lebanon, Iran, and many other places in Africa to different ones, reversing verbs, rearranging sentence structure, and even changing the horoscope. There is a big section for girls, and one page for *ce-liberat-ions*: when people liberate themselves from things they do not like and gain new freedoms.

The time comes when I publish an end-of-the-summer issue of my muse paper, dedicated to Barakat family accomplishments: Mother and I have completed the ninth grade, me with a certificate and she without. She will be able to start tenth grade, our first year of high school, along with me, except she will enroll as a full-time student at al-Urduneyyah.

Basel has finished high school and is getting ready to enter Birzeit University. He is the first one to go to college in our family, and no one can give him any advice because neither of my parents knows what college life is like. Basel has decided to study commerce. Mother sells one of her gold bracelets to help him with his first-semester tuition. After that, he must manage on his own. He will still be living at home because his college is only a short bus ride from Ramallah, and it is too expensive for him to board there.

Mona has finished the sixth grade and will enter middle school. Her school uniform will change from blue and white to green and white. Najm has turned six and will begin first grade. He is the only one in our family who writes with his left hand, and he is proud of it. Jamal, the youngest in our family, is now five years old and will enter preschool. He is already eager to be away from home. He wets his hair with water and combs it to the side, and plays at being a teacher by imitating me teaching Mother. With Jamal going to preschool, no one will need to be at home during the day, and that makes it easier for Mother to take the next big step and start attending school. But that big step comes with a big obstacle, too.

Separation

For tenth grade, I have to go to a public high school run by the Israeli government, since the UNRWA-run schools for refugees in the West Bank do not extend beyond ninth grade. I now study at Ramallah Secondary Girls School, known for its strict principal and high standards. It was originally founded by the municipality of Ramallah before the city was occupied by Israel. But now, like the rest of the public high schools in the West Bank, the school, including its staff, textbooks, and student activities, is controlled and monitored by *al-hakem al-askari*, the Israeli military governor who oversees the management of the Palestinian cities that were occupied by Israel after the Six-Day War. I must also leave Mona, who will continue at the UNRWA school and is happy that she won't be supervised by me. I am content that Mona is growing and can rely more and more on herself.

But Father has been slowly seething about Mother's studying at a co-ed school. She told him about al-Urduneyyah only after she applied and was accepted. She explained that if there was an all-girls school that would take her, she would go to it, but there isn't. Father was upset but said nothing. Since then Mother has been changing before Father's eyes; she is no longer the woman in the kitchen studying while baking bread and cooking meals for nine people every day, cleaning nonstop, and washing by hand unending piles of dirty clothes. Now she is busy sewing herself a pair of tight pants, to make herself appear closer to the age of a high school girl. She is also on a diet to lose weight so that she can look her best.

We know that Mother has always believed she looks like a movie star and wished she could be one, or at least be treated like one. She loves to speak about Zubaida Tharwat, Brigitte Bardot, Marilyn Monroe, Sophia Loren, and Elizabeth Taylor.

A big shortcoming of her marriage is that it does not give her the opportunity to dress up often and show others, women especially, how beautiful she is: her small nose, high cheekbones, thick black hair accentuating her rose complexion, coffee-brown eyes, perfectly square teeth, and small feet.

Mother teases me that my feet are bigger than hers and insists that by all standards she is more beautiful than me and Mona. When I reply that I have big feet for a big journey ahead, she raises her voice: "I am more beautiful." She also compares the shape of her face, the size of her hands, and the length of her fingers to ours. She never forgets her ability to dance.

In my heart, I know she is as beautiful as a crisp ray of sunshine in the middle of a freezing winter—hard to ignore. No one can deny that. Father is especially alert to her appearance because many men steal glances at her. While some Muslim women wear the *hijab*, my parents never speak about Mother's clothes. The idea of her covering her beauty might create a civil war in our house.

But one day after Mother has been going to al-Urduneyyah for a few weeks, Father explodes. "I refuse to let you continue to go to this school. You must quit!" he shouts. "I can't have you sitting near those men who spent time in prison, exchanging notes with them and spending hours in the same room breathing the same air! How can I show my face?"

My parents now begin to battle in a new way that is more alarming than ever before. Every word they say adds to the distance between them. "No one is going to bury my future alive," Mother says. She quotes holy sayings to support her dream. "'Seek education even if it is in China,' the Prophet Muhammad said to all Muslims, not specifying only men. Al-Urduneyyah is in al-Bireh, much closer than China!"

When Father does not agree, she takes off her gold wedding band and sets it on the table. Her face is firm like the metal and as radiant with determination. She demands a divorce, then walks out of the room.

Father stands shocked. According to our family's Islamic

tradition, it is the man who has the power to initiate a separation period or a permanent divorce. He can do so by speaking his intent out loud once, or repeating his words two or three times. But for a woman, unless her wedding agreement grants her *aaessmah*, equal-divorcing power, she cannot choose to divorce without petitioning an Islamic judge or going to a court of law to seek a legal ruling. My parents' marriage agreement does not grant Mother *aaessmah* rights.

In response to Mother's defiance, Father gathers a few pieces of clothing, packs them inside a brown paper sack, and leaves the house. He does not say where he is going. Horrified, my siblings and I try to stop him, but his expression tells us that he needs to be alone more than anything else. I pray that he will find the hope he needs in his heart, and also I ask Allah that Father not harm himself in any way. I know what the feeling of despair does to his mind.

My father is like my mother in that he has two extreme sides. He is sensitive and kind, warm and playful, yet he is also traditional and his temper can erupt beyond his control. We do not know which side will appear, or when.

As I consider that my parents are going to divorce, I am reduced to muddy confusion. In my mind I see my family about to fall like a chopped-down tree, our home split in two. It would no longer be a place where we gather for happiness or sadness. How will we continue? Who will take care of my younger siblings? How can I do well in high school exams if this trouble continues?

My parents' worlds have always been separate in some ways because of their differing educational backgrounds, abilities, ambitions, and ways of reasoning and of solving problems. They are also twenty years apart in age. But the idea that they could leave each other, or one of them leave us, is beginning to destroy even the way I write my name. My hands shake from anxiety.

Over the years, I have tried to understand my parents. Some days I thought that I grasped their differing perspectives, but now I know I am a child battling the world of grownups without understanding it. Because I don't understand, I feel betrayed by life—realizing that growing up takes years, not days or minutes.

My father ignored his illness and made himself go to work no matter what obstacles he had to face. He tried to live day by day. He thought about death as much as he thought about life. He felt lonely and abandoned when Mother did not want to join him in his view of the world. I can never begin to know Father's great burdens.

Mother fought endless daily battles to make peace with father's dangerous illness and the unpredictable life of raising children under the occupation. I can see more clearly than before what she might have felt marrying so young. It is like being thrown into the desert and asked to find her way. How painful it must have been for her to have one child after another, and be responsible for all of us every day.

But one thing remains clear to me: I support Mother continuing school. That is her right. In my mind I recite article 26 of the Universal Declaration of Human Rights, personalizing it to her: *The Palestinian woman named Mirriam who is married to the man named Suleiman has the right to an education.*

But I also support Father's need to feel a sense of dignity. He did not invent our society's conservative traditions.

"There must be a way to speak to Father so that he can hear you and remember that his dignity and yours are not different," I tell Mother.

She whips around to look at me: "You go talk to him, then!"

I feel powerless and turn away.

"I mean my words," she flares impatiently, then commands: "You. Do. The. Talking!"

So I become the ambassador between my parents.

After we find out where Father has rented a tiny room, I begin to visit him to convey what Mother says and feels. He responds, and I carry the words back to her.

I carefully consider the questions and answers they ask of and give to each other: hearing them from Mother's side, from Father's side, making sure, when I deliver them, that each word has only the good effect I hope for—that my parents will go back to each other and we will continue our life as a family. When Mother says that Father is *anany*, selfish, I delete the word and never deliver it.

She also complains about the culture, her weight, and the many women who settle for small lives and so make her appear strange for wanting to follow her dream. Mother complains so much it is as though I have ears the size of an elephant's. I do not deliver these thoughts either.

Father complains differently. He wants to tell old stories about himself and the loss of Palestine. And he has the belief that it is humiliating to tell anyone about desperate fears or feelings; he can only share those things with Allah, to whom he speaks all the time. So I realize that it is through religion that I can get Father to understand.

I offer that our first mother, Hawwa, Eve, in heaven, ate from the fruit she was curious about and for that she sacrificed living in heaven. She sought knowledge. Mother does not live in heaven. She lives in the West Bank, and also seeks knowledge. The first instruction in the Qur'an is the word *iqra'*, a command to read with the goal of gathering knowledge. It is the most sacred thing anyone can do: study. Why would he try to stop Mother from doing that?

I can see as I speak that Father loves Mother and that he admires her, too, but he feels that the occupation and the loss of our land have taken a big piece of himself. His illness takes another piece. That he cannot do what Mother is doing is making him feel not as strong or as fortunate as she is, so he is unable to see a balance in the marriage.

Father says that he will pray a hundred *rakaa*s, going on his knees before Allah, asking Him to tip his heart toward the right decision. While Father makes up his mind, I, too, must continue to search for answers.

I want to ask someone older than me, someone who also

knows my father and cares about him. Father's friends are all men and will not speak with me because I am a girl. Mother's friends would side with her. My teachers do not know my father.

The only solution I can think of is to take a trip to East Jerusalem to see the psychiatrist who gives Father his anti-sleeping pills. Father has been seeing him for many years. I will ask him not to mention my visit to Father. But when I tell Mother where I am going, she says she wants to come with me. Now my world fills with hope.

The doctor greets us and ushers us into his office. "No cure for narcolepsy yet," he says as he raises his eyebrows to show empathy and an apology. "But you can have a new bottle of anti-sleeping pills for him," he adds, thinking that we are here to get medicine for Father.

"We are here for another reason," Mother begins. "Our family is having a hard time."

He gives her his full attention.

Mother opens her mouth, but she is unable to utter a sound. The doctor is quiet.

Then she looks at me and says, "Speak for me!"

Surprised, the doctor inquires, "Does Ibtisam know what you want to say?"

"She knows the problem."

The doctor turns to me. "Tell me about your parents."

A million words rush to mind. I have no idea where to begin. "Anything?" I ask.

He nods.

I speak for a long time, and he takes notes as if I am describing an illness. Mother cries as though every word I say scrapes against an open wound. When I am done, the doctor turns to Mother and congratulates her on her courage.

He explains that we live in a time where there are prolonged hardships that lead many people to give in to despair and even to destroy their dreams. "To have a goal like you do and fight for it inspires me," he says. "But you must give your husband some of your love, in addition to your anger and disappointment. He is a brave man, and fights every moment of his day. I admire him, too. When he comes to see me for the anti-sleeping pills, he tells me how eager he is to make you happy whenever he can. Sometimes he is lost and doesn't know what to do."

I want to embrace the doctor before we leave.

Outside the clinic, Mother quietly tells me, "When you see your father, tell him to come home."

The minute we get back to Ramallah, I fly to tell Father. "Mother said, indirectly, that she loves you."

Father agrees to come back home. He and I lock our arms and walk, and with every step I wish we could dance on the street and that he could sing his joy in public.

The problem between my parents is finally over, especially because my brother Muhammad, even though it is the middle of his school year, offers to attend al-Urduneyyah, too. That way Mother will not be there by herself.

Muhammad easily thinks of others, maybe even more than he thinks of himself. If Mother demands that I eat something, he gently reminds her: "Maybe Ibtisam does not like this food. So to eat it can build her body but will hurt her soul." When my younger brothers fight like bear cubs, he separates them and reminds them that they need to help one another, not fight with one another.

Father agrees to Muhammad's offer. But he also asks Mother to promise not to look men in the eyes when speaking with them. "That is how problems happen: a look, a smile, a meeting, and then a falling..." he warns. She promises.

Because Muhammad is tall and big, and Mother appears young and does not want her classmates to know that he is one of her seven children, she tells them that Muhammad is her stepson. When I visit her school, she introduces me as her stepdaughter. I go along with it. When I speak with anyone from her school I refer to her as my stepmother. She is pleased. She exchanges her wedding ring for another, with a new, fashionable style. By the end of her first year at al-Urduneyyah, she no longer wears it to school.

When she is seen walking with Father, she says he is her father, not her husband. Those who don't know them believe this because of my parents' age difference. Surprisingly, Father does not mind Mother saying this. He tells me that he understands that she is trying to adjust to the world as a schoolgirl. "But if someone who thinks that I am her father comes to me asking for her hand in marriage, don't blame me if I make them regret every word," he says.

"I promise that I will not blame you," I reply, laughing.

Mother passes her tenth-grade exams. These results determine whether she will be placed in the *adaby*, literary, or *elmy*, scientific, stream. The topics of study and future possibilities of work are widely different in these two areas. Mother is placed in the literary stream. My own results qualify me for science.

Mother is annoyed with her results because now she and I will not have the same curriculum. We will share only Arabic, English, and religion, the core subjects required of all students. And not to qualify for the *elmy* is viewed negatively by everyone in the West Bank. The science students feel proud and are celebrated in a way that the literary students never are. Most scholarships to go to college and pursue higher education are awarded to science students. When someone says *adaby* the tone of voice is always humble, as though saying it is a failure of some sort, or that the person was not clever enough to be in science. I do not know why this is, especially because Palestinians never stop quoting poetry and literary passages with great admiration.

But Mother and I agree that this difference is meaningless. "Do you think al-Mutanabbī, the great Arab poet, and Plato, the Greek philosopher, and Shakespeare, the great English dramatist and poet, were failures because they did not do science?" I ask her.

She adds that if science is so much better than literature, then why did Allah send holy texts with nothing but stories to people, rather than sending scientific equations and geometrical shapes.

As Mother has been progressing and changing at al-Urduneyyah, Basel has been progressing and changing in college, but not in the expected academic direction. He now talks about girls all the time and brings American tourist women to visit us. They sit and we make tea for them. "American women do not care about how new or old our furniture looks," he says. "They do not care about appearances."

"But they care about your appearance," Muhammad teases.

I can see that Muhammad is especially anxious about losing Basel to a world Muhammad knows nothing about. Basel and Muhammad have been close all their lives, going to the same schools, having many friends in common, having the same summer jobs, playing sports on the same teams, and fighting against the same bullies.

But now Basel's going to college, and his interest in women, flashy clothes, and dance moves separates them and they grow apart. These are not things that Muhammad cares about. He is more like Father, quiet, seeking a secure world that only Allah can provide. Like Father, Muhammad prefers older social traditions to change.

Basel rents a post office box in Birzeit to correspond with the American women he meets. He wants to stay in touch after they go back to the States, and he does not want the letters to come to our home address. If they did, Mother would open them, ask me to translate them, and then tease Basel about the content of the letters. Basel shows me some of the adoring letters women send to him, how they compliment him and long to see him again.

Basel also goes with his college friends to other cities we have only heard of, and he spends nights out. When he is home, he plays loud Western music at the highest volume. And like many other college students, he writes letters to English-language radio programs, requesting that they play his favorite songs. He has songs by Demis Roussos, Donna Summer, Pink Floyd, Boy George, and the Eagles dedicated to his friends, and sometimes to me. I begin to write to those radio programs, too, wanting to hear my name mentioned.

As Mother and I begin the eleventh grade, Basel becomes obsessed with cars and bodybuilding. He does not own a car but has learned to drive friends' vehicles. Our walls are filled with magazine pictures of bodybuilders from around the world. And when lifting weights, he gazes at a big poster of Austrian bodybuilder Arnold Schwarzenegger.

Muhammad begins to train in bodybuilding, too, and tells me that he has quit smoking. He works hard and his muscles become well-defined like Basel's. But I know that Muhammad remains shy. If Muhammad had a choice to be on stage with a thousand people cheering at his feet or in a small garden with one bird singing, he would choose the garden and he would be patiently imitating the bird to keep it company.

Because stepping outside the house means someone, a potential admirer, will see him, every morning Basel pays great attention to his hair, buying special Head & Shoulders shampoo and conditioner. Anyone who touches his hair products must be ready for a fight with our resident Arnold. After washing his hair, he pats it dry as though every hair is an eyelash. While he combs his hair and studies his face in the only mirror in the house, I braid my hair without a mirror.

After Basel sees the movie *Saturday Night Fever*, he begins to act like John Travolta, spending every minute in the house practicing dance moves with a shirt unbuttoned down to his navel, a gold necklace lost in his chest hair, bell-bottom pants, and long bangs that he tosses right and left to cover his eyes. He dances harder than Mother studies.

Then one day in the early spring, Basel announces he is going to move to America. Someone he met during a part-time job he had as a money changer will sponsor his travel and give him work in Chicago. He will go to a country that is open and filled with freedom.

With all the preparation for his leaving, our house fills with a strange sadness, especially because we have no idea what America is like, and any Palestinian who leaves the borders is not guaranteed reentry.

People visit us to say goodbye to him on the last day, all remembering sons they have lost to the most painful word in the Arabic language, *ghurbah*: leaving home and going to live far away in a world that is unfamiliar. One becomes a *ghareeb*, a stranger.

Grandma, as she looks at Basel, remembers Grandpa, who decided that *ghurbah* anywhere is easier than living under occupation. He offered to take her with him, but she said she couldn't leave her homeland no matter who ruled over it. They separated, and Grandpa settled in Belgium.

Now Basel stands at the door with a small suitcase, wearing shiny shoes, a smile in his eyes. He is ready to go. Because I have many pen pals, he hands me the key to his post office box in Birzeit as a gift. I will no longer need to receive my correspondence at home, where Mother insists I tell her what is written in the letters.

Father weeps. "Let me look at you and fill my eyes with you before you leave," he says. He holds Basel's face between his hands, kisses him on the cheeks, and embraces him in a way meant to last him for years. He places his head against Basel's chest and laments: "There is no future for us on our land. We have to go away to make anything of ourselves. *Allah maa-ak*, may Allah be with you," Father says as Basel walks out the door of our house for the last time. Father's tears pour for days.

Shortly after we learn that Basel arrived safely in America, Muhammad decides to leave school. He says he is taking time off to work and become more independent.

"Don't do that!" I plead with him. "Finish school first. You only have a few months left. Consider it a prison sentence and finish. Don't stop just before the end. What is independence without education?"

"I'm not prepared to sit for any exams," he says, looking discouraged and tired.

"Please finish high school first. Without finishing, all the work you've already done will be lost."

Muhammad does not change his mind: he leaves school. And he says nothing about Mother continuing to go without him to al-Urduneyyah. He also stops his bodybuilding. Without Basel, Muhammad appears lost. He goes back to smoking.

I ask him what work he will do, and he says he can work on a construction site and that will be some sort of bodybuilding exercise. He tells me he also wants to get his driver's license.

Without Muhammad going to school with her, Mother announces that it is necessary for us to move again—this time to a place closer to her school so that she can walk a shorter distance. More important, because she and I no longer study the same subjects, she wants to have a guest room, for inviting her girlfriends Abla and Athena to come to our place and do homework together. She wants to live in the center of Ramallah.

To meet the extra expenses of the move, Mother takes part-time work as a seamstress working for Ramallah's mayor's sister. She will help her with special projects: mainly making dresses for brides from wealthy families.

The minute we learn that an apartment has become available in the Salah Building on Main Street, the first commercial housing project in Ramallah, my father signs the lease. How wonderful it will be to live in the center of the city.

PART IV

Main Street
1980–1981

People

We move at the beginning of June, just after school ends. The first morning in the new apartment, I am still in bed, even though it is eight-thirty, when our doorbell rings many times, nonstop. I jump up to answer it. Randa, our next-door neighbor, is standing there looking afraid and shaking her hands in the gesture Palestinians use to express that something terrible has happened.

"Did you hear? Turn on your radio," she says.

We do, and learn that only ten minutes away from where we live, Ramallah's mayor, Karim Khalaf, is fighting for his life. This morning, when he started his car, a bomb that had been planted in the engine exploded. Another bomb went off when he took his foot off the brakes. Then a third exploded seconds after one of the mayor's neighbors pulled him out of the car.

I stand on the balcony of our new apartment for the first

time and look down at Main Street below us. Army jeeps are speeding past to other parts of the city. Shopkeepers are coming to work holding their portable radios to their ears. A military helicopter hovers above.

Then we hear that twenty-three miles away, in the city of Nablus, north of Ramallah, there was another car bombing that damaged both of its mayor's legs.

Who and what next? The question is on everyone's mind. Shortly after, we learn that the mayor of al-Bireh is the third target. But having heard about the two injured mayors, al-Bireh's mayor sought help before entering his car. An Israeli explosives expert rushed to neutralize any bombs in the mayor's vehicle. But he did not consider the possibility of danger outside the car. As he opened the mayor's garage door, a bomb went off and caused the explosives expert to lose his eyesight.

The West Bank swells with pain. The Israeli government's recent decision to allow armed Israeli settlers to take Palestinian property and build two large settlements in the city of al-Khaleel, Hebron, amid the all-Palestinian population, had led to today's events. A month ago, angry Palestinians in Hebron killed six Jewish settlers. The Israeli army imposed a curfew on the Palestinian residents of the city for sixteen days. During the curfew, Israeli settlers roamed the streets, vandalizing cars and breaking windows. The Palestinian mayors of Hebron and the neighboring town of Halhoul, in addition to Hebron's Islamic religious judge, were arrested and their heads were covered with cloth sacks so they could not see where they were being taken. They were left at the Lebanese border and ordered not to return.

An armed Jewish extremist group called Gush Emunim is connected to this morning's explosions.

Over the next few days, from my perch on the balcony, I watch the protests. Then, to prevent any new confrontations, Israeli soldiers impose a curfew on Ramallah. But that does not help and only adds to the volatile feelings.

In this new apartment with the balcony over Main Street, a curfew is different from before. Instead of the army watching us from towers and rooftops, we are now the ones doing the watching from above. From the balcony we can observe every move of the soldiers on the street, especially those in open army jeeps who chase boys staying out in spite of the curfew.

When soldiers see us looking, a few of them point their guns at us. Snipers take the stairs all the way to the tops of high buildings, including ours, to monitor the streets below. We hear their footsteps. They enter some homes randomly to show that they are in charge, and special units search homes where they suspect protesters are hiding. They always work in groups because they are afraid families will make a surprise attack on them. The curfew lasts five days, but the protests last for weeks.

In the middle of the summer, Ramallah begins to return to normal in spite of the snipers who seem to live on top of the taller buildings. We try to ignore them and go on with our lives.

Instead of working in a factory this summer, I teach Arabic to children of foreign families who have come to Ramallah to do missionary work, help the UN agencies, or teach in private schools. I also tutor high school students who have gotten incompletes in some of their classes and will only advance to the next grade level if they pass the course by the end of the summer. Tutoring helps me earn some money and distracts me from my worries and fears.

Encouraged by my working, Mona gets a part-time job selling eyeglass frames. Some days she comes home wearing green or blue contact lenses and we hardly recognize her. She looks like a cover girl from a European fashion magazine.

In the late afternoon after work, observing the endless changing images we see from our balcony becomes the perfect escape for Mona and me and our younger siblings. Mother writes ten balcony ground rules, all beginning with the word *no*: no climbing; no standing on chairs; no waving to friends, or anyone, even if they wave to you; no spitting on passersby; no shouting; no dropping shoes on people's heads "accidentally"; no wearing skimpy clothes; no combing hair; no throwing things on the street; and no smiling at boys. Following these instructions makes us feel like we do not have a balcony. So we follow them only when Mother is watching.

My younger brothers bring chairs and stand on them. They dangle strings as though fishing and are happy when the strings reach people's heads or go all the way down and touch the sidewalk. They fly paper airplanes over the side of the balcony. They float balloons. They play a game in which one of them sneaks out of the apartment and goes down to the street so the other can drop a walnut or a piece of candy for him to catch inside a brown bag or small bucket. People passing by wonder what my brothers are doing.

On the first floor of our building, there is a liquor store owned by a man named Zaghroot. Liquor stores are frequented by the many Christian residents. Ramallah Muslims who drink alcohol, however, try to hide their drinking; to make the shop appear innocent, Zaghroot has a big stand of chewing gum, KitKat, and Mars candy bars near the entrance.

Next to the liquor store, there is a billiard hall also owned by Zaghroot. Once, two men darted out into the street holding pool cues like wooden swords as they clashed and swore. Mona and I dropped a trickle of water on their heads. They looked up and didn't see us, but they stopped fighting.

Across the street from us, there is a stretch of shops that includes Halweyyat Demashq, Damascus Sweets. Every hour the boy working there pours syrup on a huge tray of freshly baked *kunafah*, nearly everyone's favorite pastry in the West Bank. When the boy plays popular songs loudly as he works, we hear the music clearly and hum along as we do our housework.

Next to the pastry shop is the barber. His name is al-Hen. He looks like an ancient white-haired lion who chain-smokes. Every few hours, a man walks in to get his hair cut. Al-Hen drapes a sheet on the customer and flies around him with scissors and a comb. When the customer leaves, Mona and I give the haircut a score from one to ten. We wish this were a women's hair salon so that we would see more appealing hair art.

Farther down Main Street is Abu Iskandar's stand. He sells *shawerma* sandwiches, the Arabic version of the Greek gyro. With only one small table and two chairs, people mostly stand on the curb to place their orders and eat. He also sells sheep- and goat-brain sandwiches. When he slices the brain, it is as soft as cream cheese, and he spreads it on pita bread. High school students joke that if you eat brain sandwiches you'll do well on Tawjihi exams. I ate one once to see what a brain tastes like. It was like a bland cream.

Kishshik, right next to the *shawerma* stand, is one of the many gold shops on Main Street. Gold shops are extremely popular because girls have the main part of their marriage dowry in jewelry. So each shop is filled with charms made of 24-karat gold—hearts, snakes, pears, flowers, girls' names, zodiac signs, the name Allah, alphabet letters, crosses, and Qur'ans. There is also a one-inch-map charm of historic Palestine before it was renamed Israel. Many girls wear this map, and it is the only inch of Palestine they can take with them wherever they go. I do not have any pieces of gold since I lost the earrings Mother gave me in the first grade. I wear rubber or yarn bracelets and a piece of tape with drawings on it for a ring.

The most famous shop on Main Street is Rukab, the ice cream shop where my brothers purchased ice cream to sell during the summer. It is so famous that Main Street is nicknamed Rukab Street.

Right across from Rukab is one of the most annoying spots for girls and women in Ramallah. Here, many high school and college boys stand as though they are fashion runway commentators and evaluate out loud the clothes, shape, hair, height, and looks of every girl and woman who walks by. They whistle, shout praise, and throw love letters written on napkins or folded pieces of paper; sometimes they are mean if they do not like a girl. They act as though girls and women are there for their free entertainment.

The number-one attraction for Mona and me is Cinema Dunia, the building next to ours. Mona and I are forbidden by our parents from entering the theater without one of them with us. My brothers, sister, and I are not allowed to enter the billiard hall at any time.

When new movies arrive, Mona and I watch the man who stands on a ladder gluing the posters of actors and actresses to the wall: Najla' Fathi, Su'ad Housni, Noor al-Sharif, Hassan Youssef, Mahmoud Yassin, Hussein Fahmi, and many others. The posters always say: *Coming soon to this theater.*

But, Mona and I agree, we have a live theater below us. We have memorized details about many people who appear every day on the street going to work in the morning and then coming home in the afternoon or night. We can tell who they are by what they wear, how they tilt their heads, and how they carry their bags, hunch their backs, walk slowly, or hurry. We give them funny names based on their most pronounced characteristic. Abu Shaar Mkanfash, Father of Messy Hair;

Mashyet Tawoos, Peacock Walk; Na-ameh Bkaaeb Aalee, Ostrich in High Heels; Um Ghurrah Taweeleh, Mother of Long-Hair Bangs.

One of my favorite people on Main Street is Abdel Noor, the owner of a bookshop across from Rukab. He is an old man who always dresses in a three-piece suit. He wears thick glasses and has a gentle smile.

Even though we are friends, he never asks about my father, my mother, my siblings, my age, my grades, my address, or my religion. I never ask him personal questions either. I know that he is Christian because there is a cross on the shop's inner wall. Muslims in Ramallah put verses from the Qur'an on their walls instead.

At first glance you would never notice that Abdel Noor's right arm is paralyzed. I am curious about his arm, and his limp, too. I want to know if he was injured during a war. I am also curious whether he has children, because he appears older than my father, but he never mentions a son or a daughter.

From the first visit I made to his bookshop, searching for stationery, special pens, fragrant erasers, and fun greeting cards to send to my pen pals, Abdel Noor and I have spoken about art, books, news, and Ramallah history, always in humor. Often he surprises me with special publications he saves for me.

Dreams

"*Marhabah!* Hello!" I say to Abdel Noor as I offer him the tiny bag of freshly roasted almonds I bought for him to say thank you for the time he spends talking with me about the world.

"*Ahlain*, two welcomes," he responds, with the common reply to my greeting.

Abdel Noor has all three West Bank daily newspapers in front of him. Their names are *Al-Quds*, Arabic for Jerusalem; *Al-Shaab*, the people; and *Al-Fajr*, the dawn. I pick up one and skim a few lines from the front page. He volunteers the headline topics: "The Soviet invasion of Afghanistan, American hostages in Iran, civil war in Lebanon, and more militant settlements on the West Bank...I will stop here. One more thing and it is doomsday," he says.

Then he reaches into his drawer under the counter, pulls out a magazine, and sets it on the glass case. He puts his hand on the cover, trying to hide it and surprise me, but I know instantly.

"*Al-Arabi*!" I cheer. I have read old issues of this magazine that people had saved for two decades, dating back to years before the closure of borders that followed the wars. The closures prevented all publications printed in the Arab world, including books, magazines, and newspapers, from reaching us in the West Bank.

"You can keep it for three days! A friend who traveled to Jordan brought it back to me as a gift, and I have not read all of it yet."

I promptly write down the day, the hour, and the minute on a piece of paper and next to it print: *Ittifaq*, agreed! I sign my name. The clock is now ticking.

On the street, at home, on the balcony, in bed, I read and read about the diverse geography of the Arab world: al-Rubuaa al-Khalee, the Empty Quarter, the world's largest desert, located between four Arab countries; Nahr al-Assi, the Orontes River, in Lebanon, which flows in the opposite direction of other rivers in the Middle East; Jabal al-Sheikh, Mount Hermon, between Syria and Lebanon, which has snowcaps all year round. The essays and full-page photographs also explore the ethnic composition of the Arab world, which is as rich and rooted in ancient history as the geography is. I am struck by a photograph of two men rubbing noses. The caption explains it is the way people greet each other in several nomadic North African desert tribes called al-Tawareq, where men veil their faces and women do not.

I absorb every word as if I were the writer of each story. I imagine my name in print under an essay about Ramallah, describing the places, people, and events I see around me. The writers of *Al-Arabi* must be paid for their writing; maybe I could be, too.

I read the magazine in two days, not three, and having filled a notebook of thoughts related to its content, I now study the inside cover information: it is an illustrated monthly cultural magazine, founded in 1958, directed to every reader in the Arab world and every reader of Arabic in the world. Under that, I gaze at the photograph of its current editor, Ahmad Baha' al-Din. I copy his address, located next to an invitation for readers to send him letters.

That very moment, I begin composing my letter to Mr. Baha' al-Din. First I praise the content of the magazine and the striking photographs. I write that the English word *magazine* is taken from the Arabic word *makhzan*, storehouse, and *Al-Arabi* is a storehouse of exceptional information.

Then I offer to become a correspondent from a closed area, reasoning that *Al-Arabi* writers and photographers cannot enter the West Bank where I live. I could write an article about an imaginary tour of Ramallah and Jerusalem.

I also introduce myself to Mr. Baha' al-Din and give the reason I am eager to contribute to *Al-Arabi*. I talk about my people being refugees in our own home, about feeling the world does not see us, and how all the loss we have been experiencing makes us feel that we always have to be ready to lose more.

Because I know nothing about Mr. Baha' al-Din, I find myself writing openly to him.

I tell him I will complete high school next year, but I can only go to college if I pass the Tawjihi exam and get a scholarship. Even with that, there will be many expenses. My parents cannot afford to help me, so I must work. If I could, I would choose to be a writer because it is my number-one love. I sign my letter.

After I return the magazine to Abdel Noor, I hurry to the post office and ask if there is a way to send a letter from the West Bank to Kuwait. Amal, the only woman who works at the Ramallah post office, says that there is, but it would be indirect, not guaranteed, and costly. "A response to a letter mailed this way is not likely," she warns.

"I would like to try, no matter how uncertain the outcome," I say.

Amal details the necessary steps: Address the envelope and place it inside another larger envelope addressed to the postmaster in England. Also place sufficient international postage stamps and a short letter inside the larger envelope requesting that the British postmaster use the stamps to mail the letter to Kuwait, so it will appear as if it came directly from Europe.

"Remember," she warns, "on the return address you give to the Arabs you are writing to, do not write the word *Israel*; the Arabs will become upset to see it and might not write back. For them Israel is a painful name. And do not have the Arab sender write the name *Palestine* on the coming letter either; the

Israelis will become upset to see *Palestine*, and the letter will not be delivered. For them the name *Palestine* is painful. Write nothing for a country, maybe just *The West Bank* or *The Holy Land*, then wait and see. Please let me know if it works."

I follow the directions and mail the letter. When I tell Abdel Noor, he says it will be magnificent if Mr. Baha' al-Din invites me to send articles to publish in *Al-Arabi* for everyone in the Arab world to read.

I raise my hands to the sky with a smile and a hopeful prayer.

Relative

The first week of school I make a promise to myself:

Every day and every hour I shall remember that I cannot stop people from fighting and dying, and cannot do anything about Iraq and Iran, the American hostages, Lebanon, the civil war and the Palestinian camps, the PLO, Ireland, Spain, Africa, Russia, America, and the Israeli settlers, but I can study for Tawjihi, and I will do that.

I also try to avoid the new tension in our house. Muhammad still doesn't want to go back to school, preferring to work odd jobs on construction sites. "You once liked reading books, taught me what you learned, and wanted to compete with me for good grades. What happened to make you avoid finishing high school?" I press him. He does not want to tell me and changes the subject.

And Mother has asked Father to help in the kitchen. "You can drive a truck and build a house, but cannot fry an egg?" she challenges him.

He raises his eyebrows, then tries cooking. But he mixes everything up so that Mother has to step in to save the meal.

"Why do I have to be your Boxer?" she complains.

"Who?" he asks.

"Boxer, the workhorse from *Animal Farm*," she replies impatiently.

Father has never heard of *Animal Farm*, which is a required text for both Mother and me this year, so I explain it to him. Father finally learns to fry an egg and even prepare an omelet and simple meals for himself. Rather than feeling neglected by Mother, he is proud to arrange his food on a tray and carry it to the balcony to eat and watch people. He looks like he is at a restaurant.

"I knew you could do it," Mother teases him. She feels a triumph and whispers to me that having a husband is like having an extra child; the woman has to go on teaching him how to take care of himself.

One day when I am in math class scribbling numbers, there is a knock on the door and then Sitt Salwa, the principal, enters. Her gaze scans the room from right to left. When it reaches my seat, our eyes meet. She beckons: *Come with me!* I quickly weave between the seats and backpacks on the floor. Usually only teachers speak to students unless it is something urgent. That is why I am especially alarmed to have been summoned by the principal.

Following Sitt Salwa to her office, I am certain that no one envies me. Aloof and demanding, our principal makes her daily announcements at the top of the stone stairs facing the school's playground, where we gather in the morning. There, she delivers only serious news: the beginning and ending dates of holidays; a change of teachers; the immediate canceling of the school day, which happens unexpectedly because of clashes between demonstrators and the army that ended in a curfew; and, most anxiety-provoking, the unfolding news about how to prepare for the Tawjihi exams.

When Sitt Salwa and I reach her office, she explains, "One of your relatives is waiting on the playground. You may be excused for the day if needed." She then puts on her reading glasses, pulls a stack of papers close, and motions for me to go.

That a member of my family is on the playground at this early hour of the school day is the last news I want. Who might be there, and why? The principal used the masculine noun, so I conclude that the person is not my mother. I ask if the person is wearing a *hatta wa egal*, because my father does not leave the house without his traditional head cover.

"No," she replies without looking at me.

Now I wonder if my father has had an accident and someone is here to tell me. This is my biggest fear.

"Don't expect the worst!" the principal suddenly says as she notices my reluctance to go to the playground. *"Roohee shoofee shoo sayer. Allah maa-ek,"* she says. Go find out the news. May Allah be with you!

I am surprised by the gentleness of her voice and think that perhaps she cannot let many girls see this side of her. Encouraged by her compassion, I venture out.

On top of the steps, from where Sitt Salwa delivers her daily speeches, I look across the playground. There are three palm trees, and a man is waiting near the tallest one. He is wearing a bright white shirt under his suit jacket. Moving closer, I am certain I have never seen him before.

"You are here to see me?" I ask.

"Let me first say that we have not met before. Your relative in Kuwait requested that I carry an *amana*, a gift, for you. He wanted to make certain that you receive it by hand."

"My relative in Kuwait?" I reply, as though I'm in a dream and do not understand the story. But only a few seconds later, I am thrilled because I have figured it out.

"You are speaking of Ahmad Baha' al-Din? The famous writer?" I ask.

"Baha' is proud of you," the stranger says. "He praises you as an excellent young writer. Writing must run in the family!"

I accept the praise gratefully. The stranger then continues his dreamlike news: "A few days ago, Baha' and I met at a gathering for Arab thinkers in Jordan. He knew that I would be coming home to the West Bank. My name is Munther Salah.

I am the president of al-Najah National University in the city of Nablus."

I nod as though I've known Mr. Baha' al-Din all my life and he is my actual relative. Dr. Salah reaches into his pocket and pulls out a rolled envelope. "For you from Baha'," he says. "A letter from Baha' will follow. I dropped it off in the mailbox at the Allenby Bridge separating the East and West Banks. The extensive searches and questioning that happen there make it impossible to carry a letter to anyone. But expect to get it maybe in ten days, maybe in ten weeks. I certainly hope it arrives soon."

"If I walk there and rest every five minutes, I would get there in less than ten days," I protest.

Dr. Salah smiles. "Do not be surprised if the letter arrives having been opened," he says. "Anything before I go?"

"Will you see Mr. Baha' al-Din again soon?"

"Perhaps next year, if I can get permission from the Israeli authorities. If you need any help, however, I have promised Baha' that I will help you to the best of my ability. Please do not hesitate to contact me." Dr. Salah then gives me his phone number on a piece of paper.

Having finished his mission, he turns around and exits through the huge metal gate that separates my school from the street.

As I return to math class, I see Sitt Salwa standing by the door of her office. I say that all is well but I am requested at home.

She nods and comments, "So this important man *is* a relative of yours!" Her voice speaks the kind of respect I wish were extended daily to all people, especially teenagers and children.

Math is ending. I clutch my schoolbag, ready to go. Everyone asks why the principal took me to her office. "One atom of mascara is seen on one of my eyelashes, and I need to go home and wash it for the rest of the day," I joke. When pressed further I announce, "I must go home because I have learned everything there is to know."

Everyone laughs.

I assure my classmates that no one died and no one was born today in my family, because I want to make certain that none of the girls stop by our home to offer condolences or congratulations after school later.

In my heart, however, I am feeling great wonder: A man who is the president of a university and whom the principal thinks is important came to give me a gift! And someone who is a famous writer, to whom I wrote a letter only a month ago, responds to me by sending a gift!

One claimed to the other that he is my relative. The other claimed to the principal that he is my relative. What a giant lesson on the theory of relativity!

At Ramallah Club, the restaurant nearest to my school, I find a perfectly hidden table and chair under a big jasmine bush profuse with white blossoms. I sit and order a cup of mint tea. When the waiter leaves I open my gift.

What I see leaves me mesmerized: a roll of money. The word

Kuwait is printed on the top banknotes. Under the Kuwaiti bills I discover Jordanian money that I recognize because in the West Bank we use the green Jordanian dinar as well as the red Israeli lira. I also find American dollars and, under the dollars, British pounds.

I look around to see if anyone notices what I am holding in my hands, but the restaurant is empty at this time of day.

Overwhelmed with the unexpected gift, and uncertain what to do next, I begin writing all that comes to mind in my math notebook until I've filled the blank pages. When I'm done, I rub my hands on the money, wondering how many and whose fingerprints I am touching and in what countries the money circulated before reaching me.

I decide not to go home until school is over, so I run to Abdel Noor's shop to share the news with him.

"No school today?" Abdel Noor says, glancing at my uniform.

"There is. But I had to leave early. How are you?"

"Pondering the world," he says, smiling.

"May I add a happy piece of news that perhaps can change your view of the world for one minute?"

"Hmmm."

"Remember that letter I wrote to the editor of *Al-Arabi* magazine?"

"Of course!"

"I received the reply today."

"*Alf mabrook*, a thousand congratulations," he cheers.

"The editor sent me a gift, and a letter from him is on the way."

I show Abdel Noor the money. He gasps and adjusts his thick glasses to make certain that what he sees is right. "All of this is a gift! And in Kuwaiti cash?"

"Not only Kuwaiti." I show him the other bills.

He praises the Virgin Mary, then holds out his left hand to shake my right hand, his eyes shining with friendship. If his right arm were not paralyzed, he might have clapped and cheered in excitement. "Promise me you will go on writing no matter what the editor's response is to your offer to write articles for the magazine," he encourages.

"I promise, but only if you sell me the best paper, good stickers to put on my envelopes, and a Parker fountain pen. I think I can now afford one."

"Parker! It is the pen of a real writer. To write with it, one must slow down as though each word is meant for eternity," he says, mimicking the pen's television advertisement. "The Parkers are parked over here with different-colored ink jars, too, anytime you want to price them."

Now, judging by the clock on the bookshop's wall, half an hour remains until the school day is over. I must leave right away to make sure my classmates will not see me still in my uniform and wonder what I have been doing.

Walking home, I am torn between a great rush of happiness when I think of the moment I opened my gift, and the need to answer one immediate question: where to hide the money to keep it safe. I do not want to tell my family, because Father would say, "Let's spend it now and Allah will send you more for your college expenses." Mother would go on and on for a whole day complaining about how she suffers, so that I would give the money to her to buy a washer and dryer, or something to show off in front of her friends, rather than keep the money for my college tuition.

With every step I consider a different possibility for where to hide it. Then as I pass by a fabric shop, an answer becomes clear in my mind.

For three days, the money has been inside a ball of orange yarn that I unraveled from a sweater that had holes in the elbows. The afternoon I arrived with the money in my pocket, I announced that I needed a rest from books and using my mind, and wanted to do something with my hands. I then pulled out the sweater and unraveled it. I placed my treasure in the center and wrapped the yarn around it. When I was done, I knitted new rows so it would look like I was beginning a winter scarf. Planting the two needles in the sides like antennas, I left it on the table. Mother admired the speed with which I completed the task. What a relief!

This, however, is only temporarily safe. Hour after hour, when not imagining how this gift can change my life, I am thinking that I need a permanent hiding place for the money.

I decide I should see about putting it in a bank, although my parents do not deal with one and I have no knowledge of how to start. But I tell myself if my life is to be different from my parents', I must do something they have not done before.

There are no Palestinian or Islamic banks in Ramallah. There are only two Israeli banks: Leumi and Discount. I stand across the street from Leumi to watch the entrance and see who goes in and out. I am going to be late for school, but my investigation is more important. After fifteen minutes I realize that not one woman has walked in, and certainly no girls. A few Palestinian men dressed in business suits enter for a short time, then leave.

Do they only speak Hebrew inside? I wonder. Certainly someone there will speak Arabic or English since the bank is in Ramallah. So I walk in.

Employees sit behind glass panels. People quietly carry money in and out, sign papers, and converse in whispers. It is so solemn it doesn't seem like the bank is part of bustling Ramallah.

In the middle of the reception area, a man notices me and comes to ask how he may be of assistance. He thinks I am lost and looking for directions. He starts to lead me outside, but I tell him I have some questions about money.

"Are you seeking information for a school paper?" He is now impatient.

"I want to see if I can open an account."

"You must be of a certain age to open one."

"I am seventeen."

"Do any of your relatives have an account with us?"

"No."

"You have funds for this?"

I nod.

He enters a small glass booth sectioned off from the lobby and speaks to the employee sitting there. The employee comes toward me. I see that he is extremely thin. His hair is blond and his skin is so light it is almost transparent.

"Reymon," he says, introducing himself, and guides me to his office. I take the seat across the desk from him.

I explain that a relative of mine in Kuwait has sent me money to help with my education. I want to deposit some of it and take out a little bit at a time.

"Good decision," he replies.

He explains that he might be able to open a savings account for me. But since I am only seventeen, I would need my father's co-signature.

"My father does not have a savings account himself," I protest. "I am old enough!"

Reymon is not certain that he can proceed.

"I will be twenty in three years, and thirty in thirteen," I joke quietly.

He smiles.

"If the bank requires more than my signature, I cannot continue," I say as I get up to leave.

Reymon stops me and goes to talk to his supervisor. When he returns he says, "We will open an account for you."

He takes my ID card and types up a long sheet of paper with pink, yellow, and green carbon copies, saying that a minimum amount is required to keep the account open. Fees apply to various transactions, and all of it is recorded and explained on the papers he hands to me.

"Any questions?" Reymon smiles again as he taps gently on his desk with the back of his pen.

"Can I bring the money during recess time around noon?" I don't want to unravel the ball of yarn in front of him.

"Yes, we can complete the transaction then."

"What if I want all my money at once someday?"

"You may have it back with the same ease you brought it in."

Reymon and I shake hands.

I run to school and the principal stops me to ask why I am late.

"I am not feeling well, but I made every effort to make it even though I am late."

She motions for me to go to class.

In my mind I say, *I am not feeling well. I am feeling great!*

During recess, after everyone is gone, I stay in class and unwind my yarn ball to set the money free. I also take out the list of currency exchange values that Reymon gave to me. A simple calculation to know how a Kuwaiti dinar, a British pound, and an American dollar compare to an Israeli lira and a Jordanian dinar tells me that Mr. Baha' al-Din sent the equivalent of more than seven hundred US dollars.

I leave school, telling the principal I should have stayed home that day. She tells me to rest and get better quickly. I run to the bank and deposit the money in my new account, except for one hundred Jordanian dananeer. Although I do not know what I can do with this sum, I am certain I could buy the entire postcard tree at Abdel Noor's shop if I chose to.

First, however, I must give away a portion of my gift as *zakat*, alms, because in Islam when you receive income or wealth you must give some away in gratitude. I learned this from my father, who gives away a tiny amount of his income to someone in need every year. He believes that Allah blesses what remains.

There is a panhandler who wears black, covering herself from head to toe in the color that represents mourning her poverty and her shame of having to beg on the streets, and she comes to mind for today's *zakat*. She has an infant whose face is coated with dust and whose clothes are rags. She sits on the ground by al-Manara Circle, where there is a big sculpture of lions and where cars exit in six different directions. It is the busiest spot in the city, with fumes, dirt, and noise all day long—and it's the least friendly place for an infant.

I buy a small can of powdered milk and a plastic blow-up lion toy for the baby. If he worries about the lion sculptures, he can hold his own and not feel afraid. When I put the toy and can in the woman's hand with some money, she explodes in gratitude and blessings: *"Allah yateekee."* May Allah compensate you. I am the one who is grateful, imagining how much happier the baby will be playing with a toy.

Then there is a boy who always sits near them with a wooden box filled with Kiwi polish and black brushes for cleaning and shining shoes. His shoes have holes, and his face and hair are not clean. His clothes are covered with brown and black polish. He begs the better-dressed men who pass by him to give him a few minutes to clean their shoes. Anytime I see a *boyajee*, shoe-cleaning boy, my heart sinks and I want him to be in school or somewhere else with other children.

No woman ever asks a *boyajee* to shine her shoes while she stands reading the newspaper or chatting with friends like men do. So I slow down without stopping and put one dinar in the boy's box. He opens his eyes wide, not knowing whether he can offer to clean my shoes or not. "This is for you to clean your own shoes and shine them," I say. He looks at his feet and pats his shoes, giving them a kiss, grinning with excited child cheer.

For my last *zakat*, I go with my father on the weekend to the *hesbeh*, the main farmers' market, in Upper Ramallah. The carts carrying every kind of fruit and vegetable have colors beyond any painter's dream. The canvas of the ground under our feet, however, is nothing but a sheet of mud. The *hesbeh* is crowded, and when we are done and away from the market, I tell Father that while he was shopping, I found fifty Jordanian dananeer, rolled up like a cigarette. I hand him the money.

He is ecstatic as he moves his eyes between me and the money. "I am sorry for the person who lost this, especially if they have a big family to support," he says. "Where exactly did you find it?"

"In the middle of the crowd. And I think that it is meant for you to have," I say. "What will you do with it?"

"First I will ask Allah to make certain that the person who lost the money finds an equal amount. Then I will buy a dinner for the family from the best kabob place in Ramallah. And for your mother I will get the best bottle of perfume."

I have tears of happiness. Mother always asks for good perfume, but Father gets her inexpensive brands. She does not open them. She wants a bottle of Chanel. I will show him where to get one.

Day by day, I am getting more accustomed to the new feeling in my life of having a bank account. In the back of my mind, however, I have been thinking about the promised letter that Dr. Salah dropped in the mail for me at the bridge.

Every time I go to open my post office box and don't find it there, I wonder if I will ever receive it. But I continue to go and look, hoping that I will.

Poetry

When the letter finally arrives I am breathless as I read the sender's name: Ahmad Baha' al-Din. On the steps outside the post office, I hover over the letter. I turn it over and see the sentence stamped on the side stating that it has been opened for official reasons. Someone I do not know has read my mail before me. But just as when I see this stamp on some of the letters from my pen pals, I stop myself from dwelling on it, focusing instead on finally having received my mail.

I open the envelope, and inside there is a card embossed with a big purple flower. The card is the size of a small notebook; Abdel Noor's shop does not have anything like it.

Neatly folded into a square inside the card is transparent airmail paper, resembling the tracing paper I use for copying and memorizing maps for geography tests. I unfold it.

Ahmad Baha' al-Din's handwriting is the first surprise. It is so small, and the contrast with the size of the card makes me laugh. As I read slowly, out loud, any anxiety I had felt about him being famous is replaced by happy anticipation:

> *Dear Ibtisam,*
>
> *I am an editor of a magazine that reaches over a million readers; I receive much mail. I read it all and appreciate every writer. Due to time constraints, I only reply to a few. But I read your letter many times and carried it in my pocket for days, hoping to find a way to reach you with an answer. I felt that my best chance was to give my response to someone returning to the West Bank who could send it from there. I also kept thinking about how determined and brave you were to manage to send me a letter from beyond the postal barriers that keep Ramallah as far from Kuwait as the moon! I have not received letters to the editor mailed from Ramallah to Kuwait before now.*

Mr. Baha' al-Din's words bring tears to my eyes. People often tell me that I am *shujaa'ah*, brave, sometimes with praise and sometimes with a hope that I will stop. *Shajaa'ah*, bravery, is a quality my culture encourages in boys more than in girls. My father does not agree all the time. "You are as good as a boy," he says. But when he wants to express his highest encouragement, he says, "You are better than a boy!"

"Boys for you are the standard of goodness?" I argue. "I prefer that when a boy does well, you tell him that he is as good as a girl."

He always smiles when I say this.

I continue reading:

> I hope you can let me know if you have received my gift. Please know that I am not a man of big wealth. I have many obligations that I must work hard to meet. I sent you the present to express my understanding of the hardship you and your people live under, and the importance of having a voice and of being heard. Writing is a most essential vein of any person's life.
>
> I have a daughter who is in college and a son in high school. I wish for you to go to college, too. I think that the responsibility of helping young people belongs with all the adults of the world, not only their immediate families and communities. In my opinion, education is the only hope, not only as a way out of economic hardships but also out of world conflicts, because with education one can find new solutions. Girls and women especially make a big difference when they continue their journey of learning.
>
> About writing, please feel free to write to me as much as you wish and keep a daily diary addressed to me if you choose to. And if you find ways to continue to reach me, and let me know more about the life of a young person in the West Bank, I will find ways to send you compensation every now

and then, whenever I can. Hardly any Arab journalist can
enter the West Bank in person. But anything you write will
give me a fresh firsthand glimpse of light into a closed world.

Please know that as a journalist I keep up daily with news
and the realities of the policies affecting your people, although
I do not live them like you do. I also know what it is to be an
exile, for I am working in Kuwait, away from my home coun-
try, Egypt, mainly for political reasons.

Under his signature he tells me to call him Baha', the name
his friends call him.

Even though he does not say whether he will publish my writing in *Al-Arabi*, I leap with joy that now I have an enthusiastic
reader, and will be paid for my writing, too. I want to shout: *I
do write every day!* Mother can testify to this. She says I am the
revenge of girls whose hearts are broken from being made to
leave school. That is, when she is not mad at my writing everywhere I can. I scribble on my hands and use my five fingers
like lines on paper. I leave notes on my clothes, especially my
pants, and on the walls and doors, and because Arabs believe
that one's destiny is written on the forehead, I write on my forehead to request good fortune.

On my way home I stop by Rafidi print shop, another one
of my favorite places in Ramallah. Many months ago, I was
pondering how to solve the problem of writing on everything

when I remembered that Nazeeh, the husband of one of Mother's friends, manages a print shop. He must have leftover paper, just like Mother always has leftover scraps of cloth. When I asked him he told me to choose what I wanted from a mountain of paper scraps. Since then, whenever I can, I have been coming home with armfuls of paper.

"When you become a famous writer, mention Matba'at Rafidi in Ramallah," he always says, smiling.

I promise to do so and say, "Mother thanks you for helping her to have fewer fights with me."

Today, striding home carrying what feels like half a tree's worth of scrap paper, I wish I could celebrate my good fortune openly with glossy cards designed and printed especially for this occasion. I would have my classmates come to my home and bring orange balloons. We would blow them up into full moons filled with unspoken dreams. We would dance gripping the strings, then release them all to the heavens. The balloons would mingle and disperse in different directions.

Mine, as I see it in my mind's eye, goes high, then turns east, leaving Ramallah, crossing the Allenby Bridge to Jordan and then on to Saudi Arabia. In fewer than sixteen hundred miles it finds Kuwait and finally lands in the hands of Mr. Baha' al-Din.

But in reality there will be no parties or even a small gathering because I am not going to tell anyone. And I hope no one notices how different I have become.

For a few days, no one says a word, but then my Arabic-language-arts teacher, Sitt Fatima, notices that for many classes I have not participated.

"*Elly makhed aqlek yet-hanna feeh*, the one who took your mind, may he enjoy the company," she says.

I am embarrassed and admit that she is right. "My Bedouin mind is wandering. If someone sees it, please let me know!"

My friend Ghada, says, "My mind saw yours half an hour ago. It was in the desert shopping for a camel."

Everyone laughs.

"I will explain more during recess," I promise Sitt Fatima.

Sitt Fatima moves on to another topic, leaving me in peace. That is one of the reasons she is my favorite teacher. Another reason is that when she speaks, she shares her love for language, hoping that we will find reasons to love it, too.

In Arabic language arts we must learn *nosoos*, selected literary texts; *qawa'ed*, grammar and sentence-structure analysis; *mufradat*, vocabulary of ancient classical words; *insha'*, creative composition; and *mahfoothat*, poetry, which is described as literature worthy of preserving permanently.

Most students in Ramallah, boys and girls, complain about these classes because they are so demanding. Changing any *harakah*, the mark placed above or under a letter in an Arabic word to guide the reader for the correct pronunciation, can dramatically change its meaning even though the letters remain the same. So careful linguistic analysis is a necessity. A sentence, and then the paragraph in which the sentence occurs, must be considered with the precision of analyzing a chemistry equation.

Because of this requirement, many students dislike Arabic class and find algebra easy compared to it. Also, many people on the streets use expressions and sentence structures that are disconnected from the original meanings. If our ancestors listened to us speak now, they would be laughing and crying.

That is why Sitt Fatima is patient. She says that forgetting our once-pioneering heritage has weakened our mastery of our culture, especially our command of our rich language, with its ancient roots.

Sitt Fatima also seems to understand the conflict between teenagers and grownups. Every day, during recess, she is the only teacher who speaks with students during her free time rather than staying in the teachers' room. We are not a burden for her. And she is excited to hear about our lives.

Even though she is kind and clever, I wonder if she is happy. Before she came to our school, she studied in Syria, then after the Six-Day War she was imprisoned by Israel for her political views. She married a famous Palestinian poet, then divorced without having children. After that, she came to teach in Ramallah and to live with her parents in her village, Kufur Ne'mah. She is the only woman in that village who drives a car.

I am so lucky this teacher came to my school and into my life. When I see her car in the parking lot, I am at ease no matter what else is happening. Instead of adding to a problem when hearing about one, like many adults do, she tries to help solve the problem.

During recess she walks toward me, adjusting her burgundy head scarf over her short hair. I must speak with her quickly before other girls join us.

"*Hatee ma endek*, show what you have," she begins.

I hand her the card and letter from Mr. Baha' al-Din, then hold myself tightly as she opens them and reads. She gasps, laughs, and quietly chirps *Ya bayye...ya bayye...* under her breath from sentence to sentence. After she finishes reading she gives me a big smile. "You have a good reason to be absentminded in class," she says. "He is one of the most respected journalists in the Arab world!"

I jump and twist in excitement. "How should I respond to him?" I ask.

"You already know what to write, because you have gotten a response!"

"I mean, something that makes me sound older..."

"*Al-haqeeqah*, the truth, is ageless," she says.

Throughout the day, I consider the word *al-haqeeqah*, truth. It is a noun with a feminine gender, not a legal expression like *al-haq*, which is a masculine noun meaning justice.

I think that the truth in Ramallah lives on the streets among our homes, and nests like birds in the tops of our trees. It is mixed with the songs we hum to ourselves when we sit alone. And because it comes out when we are alone, we are never alone. The truth is with us.

Now I ask the word itself: Dear al-Haqeeqah, tell me more about yourself. What are you? A person's pleasure? Anger? Pain? Silence? Secrets? Dreams? I put my pencil over my ear, wanting it to hear all my thoughts as I gather them before I begin my reply to Mr. Baha' al-Din, later on tonight, once Ramallah sleeps:

Dear Baha',

It is late at night. I hear the occasional careening of army jeeps patrolling the empty streets and people's dreams, and I hear the snoring of my father. To answer your question, yes, I have received both the gift and the card with the letter.

If you ask me about the happiest moments of my life, please know that you created two of them.

I am obsessed with writing, even though I am in the last year of high school and have little spare time. But writing helps me take out some of my feelings and put them aside so I have space for new feelings and thoughts. And I am never lonely because I have words. They are my confidants and companions. When I need someone to speak with, someone who really understands me, I make up a story that has that person in it, who then becomes my mind's friend.

Now I will write knowing that I can reach not only the pen pals I have around the world, but a "pen-nacle" writer in the Arab world. Thank you for encouraging and helping me to grow and continue to reach others with my words.

Ibtisam

I enclose with my reply a separate page filled with nothing but the word *shukran*, thank you. In my heart I know that the first and the last thanks are to Allah. Father reminds me always that if one says *shukran* to Allah, that means acknowledging a gift has been received and appreciated. More gifts can then be granted.

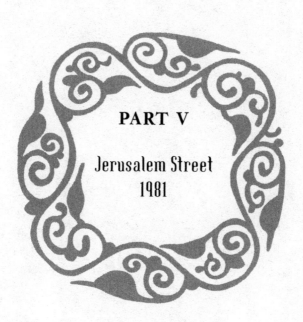

PART V

Jerusalem Street
1981

Time

It is spring vacation, only one semester to complete before the final Tawjihi exams. I am gazing at the distant hills of Ramallah, which have turned into giant waves of poppies, calla lilies, tulips, wild daisies, and dandelions. But I am thinking about a thorny problem.

This year, some of my classmates have gotten engaged and plan to get married in the summer after the exams.

Sabah says she is marrying for love and is celebrating. Feeling bolder by her changed social status, she no longer worries about what the principal thinks or says. Sabah now curls her hair, and the minute classes are over and we walk out of the school gate, she unbuttons the collar of her school uniform to show the gold necklace she received, with the engagement ring on it as a charm, and rolls up her sleeves to show her bracelets, gifts from her groom that are part of her dowry.

Farah, however, whom I have known since middle school, is mourning her engagement. She went home one afternoon to discover that her father had given her hand in marriage to a man who lives in Saudi Arabia. Her mother also agreed to this arrangement. She is the only girl in her family, with nine brothers. She has no one in her family to speak to about her problem.

Sawsan and Sonya did not get engaged, but they began to cover their hair with scarves and wear their long *hijab* on top of the school uniform. They are getting ready for a new life as observant religious women.

Dana, a girl everyone calls progressive, comes from an activist family and is going in the opposite direction. She says that she doubts the existence of God. Everyone whispers that her father is a communist and she is, too.

I avoid speaking about marriage and religion with my classmates, feeling that no one knows what is in another person's heart and mind and no one has had another person's experiences. So I believe that it isn't right to judge this way. I only listen to everyone's views.

Months ago, when questions about Allah filled my mind with doubts after my people's conditions only got worse, I knew that I could not ask anyone for an answer about God without their becoming alarmed and trying to press their views on me. So I told no one about my doubts.

I bought a big white daisy from a flower shop and sat amid the television antennas on the roof of our building. Silently, I said a big hi to Allah, thinking that I must say *high* as I looked at the blue sky. I smiled at how people would be surprised to know that I say hi to Allah as though I am speaking to a dear friend. I then asked with all my heart: *If you exist, know all things, and control all outcomes, please help me not to have any doubts about your existence.* I then began: *Allah exists*, and ripped off a petal. *Allah does not exist*, ripped off another petal. *Allah exists, Allah does not.*

My heart pounded as I got closer to the last few petals, not at all wanting the possibility that Allah does not exist. I stopped and then thought about both possibilities for the rest of the day.

Finally, I decided that Allah exists simply because that is the better answer for me. If God is not present, then that would mean only men and guns, soldiers and bullies are in charge of the future, and my prayers go nowhere. I wanted, in my mind, for Allah, who creates all the flowers of the world and all the beauty in life, to be bigger than all men, just like the daily prayer says five times a day: *Allah akbar:* God is greater than everything and everyone. I felt happy with my decision.

The continuing news of my classmates' engagements makes me wonder how any girl can do well in her end-of-year exams while thinking about marriage, too. I relate only to those dedicated to their studies and hoping to go to college, until Father announces on the first evening of spring break that the son of someone he respects is asking for my hand.

"Not possible!" I reply. "I have *one* goal between now and the summer."

"They are coming to see you, and the date for the visit is set," he says, leaving me in shock.

"It is only an engagement, nothing serious before you and I finish Tawjihi," Mother intervenes. "They are wealthy, and he speaks English. We will make sure that he agrees to permit you to attend college."

The words *wealthy*, *agrees*, and *permit* make me boil. Why must I rely on someone else instead of working? Why must I add another person to my life whose permission I need?

Many girls I know try to escape their families' strict control through marriage. They say marriage will give them more freedom. But I think they are wrong: all they will have is a different life that is more of a prison with harder labor. Unmarried girls spend many hours outside the house for school each day, I reason, so girls should delay getting married as long as they can and choose education. Besides, what are they going to teach their children if they know so little?

In my heart, I want to experience what my grandmothers and mother have not—real freedom and the ability to make decisions for myself. That is why, without knowing who he is, I am certain that this man who is coming to ask for my hand must be stopped.

Because many men in Ramallah prefer to marry girls who have long hair and who do not wear glasses, the next day I find myself at a hair salon saying one sentence as sharp as a pair of scissors: "Cut off the braid."

The hairdresser says, "Why? Who died?" She thinks I am

cutting my hair because I am in mourning. I watch my long braid fall to the floor. I pick it up and hold it in my palm for a minute before I drop it so it can be swept away. After that I buy a pair of nonprescription glasses.

When I knock at the door, Mother does not recognize me for a minute. Then she slams the door and refuses to let me enter.

"It is *my* hair," I say, "every strand of it."

She does not respond.

I wait outside for Muhammad to come home from work, thinking he may help me. But when I tell him what happened he says he has no advice to give to me. "This is your life," he says. "As for me, I am working three jobs to be able to save up some money for a ticket to leave the country."

"I want to be able to do the same," I tell him.

"But you are a girl, and our parents will never let you go anywhere unmarried."

When Muhammad fails to convince Mother to let me in, he comes with me on the bus to Grandmother Fatima's village in Jerusalem.

"Do some thinking and I will be back in a couple of days," he says. "And by the way, you look good in short hair, too," he adds, smiling.

I thank him for his support.

In the quiet of the village, I anxiously try to decide what to do to make peace with Mother before spring break is over. I do not want to miss any school days. I am thankful that Grandma does not side with my parents or with me. So after only one day I decide to go home. I agree to meet the man asking for my hand, but on one condition: I will speak to him in English when they visit us.

My parents agree. "Whatever it takes to get you closer to marriage," they say.

Opening my books, I pretend to study but instead think about boys and men and how strange their behavior is. Girls and women do not seem to create problems for men's plans and dreams. They often help them. Why do men then try to interrupt women's lives and call that love and admiration! I have never seen anyone in my family or among our relatives teaching boys and men to listen to a girl without interrupting her, or encouraging them to ask a girl about her talents and dreams and how she plans to change the world, then celebrating her desire to become a leader with her talents.

For me, even the thought of marriage before I become independent feels like a shackle around my ankle. If I do get married, I will not be able to move freely, or leave the country when the opportunity comes. Every year, Aunt Rasmeyyah, Father's sister, reminds Father that one of her sons wants to marry me. Every few months, my parents mention that someone is interested in visiting us to talk about me. But when they raise the subject I quash it quickly, like running to shut a window when a dangerous storm begins.

I have been avoiding boys, except for my pen pals, and those who are where I have worked. Some of the foreign students

I taught Arabic to, and those who had incompletes whom I helped to pass exams, are boys. But when I am the teacher, I act like a parent. I am responsible for their learning and helping them to succeed, and do not think about anything else.

I still do not have a plan for setting myself free from this man whom I agreed to meet. Mother keeps repeating the proverb that does not apply even to her own life: *The shade of a man is better than the shade of a wall.*

"Are you saying that a woman must live in someone's shade? I do not want shade," I tell her. "I like the sun, for it has all colors, and if I must stay away from the sun, there are trees and hats that can provide shade better than a man."

"His father owns a watch shop," she announces happily.

"That means he has plenty of time on his hands," I mock. "But I do not. I have something more important to do."

"We want you to marry after you are done with school so that your happiness and safety will be ensured," Mother says.

Now I am furious. "Look at how marriage ensured your happiness, Mother. I do not want to rely on a man for money or protection and I do not want a life like yours. And no one is safe on the West Bank, not a man or a woman."

"There is nothing you can do," she presses. "It is already agreed." She also says that she has made an appointment for me at a beauty salon to groom my hair and eyebrows. The next day we go, and I come home with eyebrows as thin as pencil lines.

* * *

I am on the balcony asking Allah to help me, then asking the moon and stars to shine light on this dim moment. The moon tonight is full. It has just risen above Ramallah and appears soft and smudgy, as though it has been drawn in chalk.

Mona comes to speak with me, bringing a blanket so that we will be warm. We put our feet up against the cool rails. Jamal nestles between us. He is only seven but he wants to understand everything.

"Can you believe that after all the time I spent helping Mother with school she wants me to get engaged when I need to be most focused on my studies?" I say.

"Do not be sad," Mona says. "Think of Mother as Cinderella's mean stepmom, and talk to the man. Maybe he is a prince. Maybe you will have a fairy-tale ending, where all injustice ends with fairness."

"But Mother is not a mean stepmother only. Sometimes she is a whole staircase. And she wants me to have an un-fair-y tale, with my right to self-sovereignty taken away. I must defend my dream of freedom."

"All right, forget about Cinderella. Let us pretend that we are in *Little House on the Prairie* on channel six. Didn't you say you will speak to this man in English only? I am certain that you can do something mischievous that would delight even Laura Ingalls."

"I hope you are right, Mona. And you, what do you dream of accomplishing after finishing school?" I ask.

"I have two plans. I want to become a flight attendant or a nurse." She rubs her hands in delight.

"Why?"

"Because in both professions I can wear a beautiful uniform, put my hair up neatly under a hat, and be the one in charge at important moments."

"You cannot be a flight attendant in the West Bank," I tell her. "We do not have Palestinian airlines, and the only airport we have is Qalandia, which has been out of service since the Six-Day War."

"Then that's destiny telling me to take the nursing path," she says, giggling. "But being Palestinian teaches you to be ready for any destiny."

Now we are silent for a long time.

"What if we go to different countries and cannot see each other?" she asks. "What if we are separated for years like Aunt Amina and Mother? Like Grandma and Grandpa? Like us and Basel now—not knowing when we will next meet?"

"Let us have an imaginary balcony on the moon," I say. "If we cannot see each other in person, when the moon is full, and we can see it from wherever we happen to be living, we can gaze upward, climb to the sky like we climb the staircase of the Salah Building, and meet there. If I don't find you when I get to our moon balcony, I will leave you a long letter with my news. Don't forget to do the same."

"All right," Mona replies excitedly. "I also will plant some imaginary flowers so that fragrant petals will glide from the sky to the earth on moon rays, and because we have the most beautiful family name in the world—*Barakat*, meaning blessings—I will paint a sign saying: WELCOME TO THE BALCONY OF BLESSINGS."

"I want to be there with you, too," Jamal says, reminding us that he is nestled between us and has heard everything we said. We both embrace him.

Before we go to sleep I tell Mona that I have a plan for how to respond to the man who wants to ask for my hand, but she has to wait to learn what it is.

Our guests will arrive this afternoon. My parents are different people in the presence of visitors. I ponder why strangers are welcomed with cheer, when family members are treated in ways that are often thoughtless.

To prepare for the visit I aim to look as ugly as I can. Mother sees the clothes I put on, and demands that I change into something more feminine. She picks out a dress that I refuse to wear at first but finally accept to avoid a fight. It is true that I do not want to marry. But I am certain I want to live, and Mother has the look she reserves for special occasions. We call it the RBJ look, referring to Soviet-made rockets.

Suddenly Mona rushes in from the balcony, saying that the guests are at the entrance of our building. "There are eight of them!"

Mother leaves me and goes to put on the last touches in the room where we receive guests.

I hear the doorbell ring; the minutes pass by slowly until Mother comes to get me: "The empty seat next to him is for you."

I raise my hands to the sky for divine help and follow her.

"Ma sha' Allah…" Everyone praises the Maker for my beauty. I sit next to the man who appears to be in his early twenties, not knowing what his name is. I never asked or wanted to know. On the coffee table are roasted pistachios, fresh fruit, and pastries. There is also Arabic coffee and tiny cups, which I had refused to carry on a tray and take to the guests as most girls do when someone comes to ask for their hand in marriage.

As minutes tick on the wall clock in front of me, I am more and more certain that I can solve this problem, but I am anxious and everyone sees it. To ease what everyone perceives as normal girl shyness, one of his relatives begins speaking about politics, the most common social topic of all Palestinian life after religion and food.

They comment on the American hostages in Iran, who were finally released after 444 days. They wonder if the new American president, Ronald Reagan, will do anything useful to help end the Israeli occupation.

Mother switches the topic to the engagement of Princess Diana. I know that she is reminding me to speak to the man.

I turn to him and say: "Let us speak in English."

He adjusts his posture to indicate that he is ready.

Before starting, I ask if anyone else in the room speaks English and can converse with us.

They all say no, except for Mother, who can speak some.

But I know her level of fluency, and if I speak quickly, she will not understand. So I begin.

"Your family owns a watch shop. The word *watch* in English is a verb and a noun. Are we watching time or is it watching us?!"

"Is this philosophy?" he protests without looking at me. "I do not like it. It gives me a headache."

"All right, no need for philosophy. What do you know about the history of keeping time and the science of making watches? Who invented the first *saa'ah*, the hourglass?"

"I do not know," he replies, now appearing annoyed.

That makes me feel I am succeeding in making him dislike me.

"If we marry, I will be speaking about philosophy, history, and science all the time. That is what I know and like. Besides, I do not know how to cook because questions about cooking do not interest me."

"You do not know how to cook?" He raises his eyebrows. "Most girls who do not cook pretend that they do to appear ready for marriage. Why are you telling me this?"

"Does it make a difference if you marry me or another girl?"

"Our shop is on Main Street, and I watched you walk to school and back every day for some time and decided that I wanted you."

"What if I do not want you?"

He is silent.

"I do not want to marry you. My dream is to finish school, go to college, travel, and discover the world. People say women should stay at home. But home for all people is all of planet Earth. So, *law samaht*, please, I ask that you tell my family that you do not want to marry me, because if we do marry, against my wishes, I promise"—now I take a deep breath before I continue—"to make your life miserable!"

"You must be in love with someone!" he challenges. Everyone hears the word *love* and looks at us. I get up to leave with careful steps and an averted gaze as though I am embarrassed to go on with the conversation and the talk of love.

In a week he tells Father that he did not understand everything I said to him in English, and that he wants to wait longer before choosing a wife.

"The man looked somewhat unhappy as he spoke," Father adds.

"What did you tell him in English?" Mother now demands to know every word.

"I forget!"

"*Yallah!* That is all right," Mona jokes. "Time heals all wounds. He is a watchmaker and probably knows that. Tick. Tick. Tick." She taps with her fingers on the wall where she is leaning.

My father decides to spare himself further arguments with me. He announces that he will tell anyone who asks that only after the end of the summer will he consider any proposals. I embrace him.

I am now free to go to the Tawjihi exams with nothing on my mind but my dream of completing high school with a high grade-point average. No, no. With a high grade point, above average!

Result

Only a few days are left until the Tawjihi final comprehensive examinations. Like thousands of other students I have walked miles and miles with open books between my hands, head down as I studied a page. I skipped social activities, television, many hours of sleep, and many meals. I have memorized whole books, the periodic table with all the elements, a long list of equations and proofs, Qur'an verses for religion class, hundreds of poetry lines, biology facts, intricate Arabic grammar, and English rules.

There was also a small folder titled "Arab Society and the Palestinian Problem" that was half handwritten and half typed. This is the first time in twelve years of school that we studied anything about Palestine. There were no maps in it, no flags, no mention of Palestine or Israel, no history or United Nations resolutions, no possible solutions, only a description of the problem with vague references. We are meant to copy the folder, read it alone, and not have any discussions in class about it. Many students created jokes to mock this folder and called it *sharru al-baleyyah*, the worst of a tragedy, after the Arab saying: *The worst of a tragedy is what makes a person laugh.*

The feeling about this subject is heightened by the news from Lebanon that has become difficult to ignore. The civil war in Lebanon is entering its sixth year, and this week the Israeli air force entered Beirut to bomb the PLO headquarters and the main Palestinian refugee camps there. But I tell myself that all Palestinians everywhere, even in the refugee camps of Lebanon, would want me to focus on the exams ahead.

I ask Mother in the evenings how she is doing. She complains that no matter how much one prepares, nothing guarantees the outcome. She is right, and we face many other difficulties. Our textbooks are determined by Israeli authorities, while the test is created by a testing organization in Jordan and we get a copy of the exam. So even though our textbooks are copies from the Jordanian textbooks, because when Israel occupied the West Bank it kept the same textbooks for our schools, they do not get updated because of the political tensions between Jordan and Israel. Also, some passages and references have been deleted from our textbooks by the Israeli military supervisor. We may be asked questions about subjects that students in Jordan have been taught but we have not. After the results are announced, there is no appeal process. Students who fail or who wish to take the exam again to raise their grade-point average have to repeat the school year.

And not every one of our teachers is qualified to teach in his or her field. My chemistry and math teachers do everything they can to help us learn and be ahead of other schools. My biology teacher is also helpful, although when it was time for the one-hour class on the human body, she let the principal invite a male science educator from a boys' school because she was too shy to talk about body parts.

My physics instructor has a degree in agriculture. No matter what we say to her in class, she repeats her lesson plan like a radio program that never varies. We know less after she teaches us because her confused knowledge shakes our confidence in what we thought we understood before she taught us. This leaves many of us searching for outside help.

On the first day of exam week, Mother and I are ready. The first exam subject for me is mathematics and for her is history. We have breakfast together. Open books leave little space for our plates on the table. We chew our bread and mix sugar into milk slowly as the sunrise mixes colors into the darkness, turning gray into purple into pink and red and then daylight.

As she eats, Mother prays and then says, "I must remember to breathe."

"Or you can sing," I joke affectionately.

We laugh, get ready, and then part like a pair of compasses that will draw a circle only when we come home at the end.

Arriving early with many others, I see proctors asking everyone to empty their pockets, making certain that we hide nothing we can cheat with. Some students hurry to look at their notebooks for the last time before dropping them in the book-and-backpack corner.

I have no cheat sheets hidden anywhere, for I prepared those and let go of them weeks ago. I wrote out all the information that I wanted to cheat on because I was worried about it, then studied it first, making cheating on the day of the exam unnecessary.

The proctors stand alert. Most of them are teachers who have come from other towns, cities, and villages. Our own teachers work in other centers with students whom they have not taught.

All is ready and the timer is set. The room is silent except for the proctors' footsteps along the rows, and faint grating of sharpeners against pencils. The best sharpener for the mind in this hall, however, is the mix of anxiety and excitement filling us. The doors are closed and a teacher starts the timer. Pencils then touch paper, and there is no stopping after this moment.

I glance at all the pages of the booklet to determine where best to start. Most of the sections are multiple-choice questions. We are to do the needed calculations on the back of the booklet and not use any extra paper. I write down the formulas I have memorized that give shortcuts to answers. From question to question my cheeks become hotter as though I am running a race. I only stop when one proctor leans close near my ear and whispers: "I am told that you are a good student."

At first I am puzzled. Then I understand when I notice a girl

I don't know, a few seats away from me, weeping and shaking quietly.

"Some of the students," the proctor whispers, "have not studied well enough because of hard circumstances. Will you help?" She looks me in the eye and raises her eyebrows. I know that some people cheat on exams, but I have never heard of a proctor facilitating this.

As I try to decide what to say, I remember Wafa from Beitunia and the death of her mother. She never had a chance even to be here. And I have heard of many incidents of hardship. Some high school students, mainly political activists or those who encourage demonstrations, are arrested by the army the night or the morning of the exams to punish them by depriving them of completing school that year. Those who come from poor families that cannot afford the expenses of another school year then have their dream to hang a certificate on the wall taken away. I think of Mother, whose circumstances made her wait for twenty years before she could continue.

"Come back in fifteen minutes," I say. "I must finish all of my work first."

"*Shukran*, thank you." She nods quietly as she leaves to whisper to the weeping girl. Now I solve test problems and worry whether I should do this or not. My father comes to mind. Sometimes when I ride with him in his truck, I see that when a police car is anywhere in the area, all the drivers warn each other by flashing their lights as they pass. The policeman hiding behind a bend in the road is then surprised by all the cars that move like turtles near him and the drivers who wave hello to him, too.

My conclusion is that for me to help someone on an exam like this is not cheating. It is un-cheating. Something in me says: We are made to live with no land, no country, no rights, no safety, and no respect for our dignity. The world is cheating the Palestinians, and it is cheating girls even more. To give what I know here to someone might not make her pass, for I cannot be completely certain that my answers are correct. But if I do help, one person will remember forever that the world is good and someone was willing to help her, just like I will forever remember that Mr. Baha' al-Din helped me by sending me money and encouraging me to keep writing.

The proctor is here again. I am ready to share my answers. She has a piece of paper and a pencil. I open my booklet with all the multiple-choice sections completed. She writes the numbers of the questions and next to them the letters I chose as correct. And she scribbles some notes from the proof-based solutions to non-multiple-choice problems.

She is grateful, offering me a big smile. I remind myself that one of God's attributes is *al-aaleem*, one who knows our reasoning and intents. With that, I am content.

Walking home, I pass by other testing centers, and notice that a few male students who finished early are on the streets shouting answers at the top of their lungs, hoping that those who are using all the allotted test time because they are having trouble may catch an answer to a difficult question. Some helpers are even climbing trees to be heard better. I know that they are mostly distracting those inside.

When exam week is over, I organize my books so that someone else in my family may use them later on. I wish Muhammad would use them. If he had stayed in school, he would have graduated by now.

"Is there a chance you will be doing Tawjihi anytime?" I ask him.

He shakes his head. His eyes are filled with sadness. I wish he would tell me what happened that made school a place of pain for him.

Mother refuses to make even one comment about how the tests went for her until we get our results.

To entertain ourselves, Mother and I watch the recording of *Madrasat al-Mushaghebeen* (*School of Troublemakers*) over and over again. It is an Egyptian play about students who drive their teachers and principal to the furthest edge of patience. We laugh for hours without stopping. They do exactly what we wanted to do with some of our teachers.

Then Muhammad comes home saying that he has changed his mind about traveling. Because many of the Palestinians who have left the country are not allowed to come back, Muhammad fears that if he leaves the West Bank, he may never be able to live in Ramallah or see us again. And he does not want that to happen. "I do not want to speak another language," he says. "Why should I? What is wrong with Arabic? I do not dream to be anyone else other than me. And I do not wish to add more complications to my life."

Part of me understands exactly what Muhammad says. The other part of me, which wants freedom at any cost, is why I am certain I would travel no matter whether I was allowed reentry or not, and would learn all the languages of the world if I had to.

Muhammad sits for a driving test and gets his driver's license. He does not speak about traveling anymore.

Mother distracts herself on the last days of waiting for the outcome of the Tawjihi with Princess Diana's wedding on television. All I celebrate is the news of Diana's refusal in her marriage vows to say that she will obey her prince. Love is enough, I think.

Summer is almost gone, and the day of the results is finally here. I walk to my school, sometimes rushing and sometimes going slowly. When I arrive, the first thing I learn is that one of my classmates who sat for the exams has died of tuberculosis.

Her twin sister, who also sat for the Tawjihi exam, and several other girls are standing in a circle crying. I recall that the classmate who died looked pale all the time. I am aware that we Palestinians living under occupation have meager public health services. Many people are diagnosed with diseases only after they die. But now I am also aware of how little I know about the lives of many of my schoolmates and the stories they have in their hearts, even though we have seen one another almost every day for years. Under our school uniforms, which make us look similar, are greatly dissimilar worlds. We do not ask or tell each other much about our private lives and how lonely and overwhelmed many of us feel. To pretend that all is well helps us to manage our pain and avoid feeling powerless and ashamed of the mountains of problems we live with but cannot solve.

Then I learn that my score is among the top ten percent in the region and that this grants me a scholarship for the first semester at Birzeit University, to study science.

I sit on the steps of my school, looking around to say goodbye to everything: the uniform I wore daily, the strict rules and structures, the principal, the teachers and their different personalities, and all the studying for grades and all the anxiety about tests. I also say goodbye to the bells ringing many times a day between classes. Could schools not have one minute of beautiful music separating classes instead of the annoying school bells? For certain, I am happy not to hear school bells again.

I look at the three palm trees under which Dr. Salah stood to give me the gift. Sitt Fatima's parked car is near them. I will come back again in the future to visit her and the palm trees.

On the way home, the streets are filled with a special Tawjihi song by Abdel Halim Hafez: "Wehyat Albee wa Afrahuh." He says there is no happiness that surpasses one's success. I celebrate by buying mascara and a bag of colorful balloons. As I tie some of the balloons to stop signs hoping that people will understand that as *Stop and celebrate*, I think of how sad this day must be for anyone who fails the exams but must hear this song everywhere for days.

When I arrive home, I find that Mother has taken out all her books and notebooks from the Tawjihi year, opened one book, and is reading. "I am not going to waste even one minute," she says, tears streaming down her face. I do not ask her what happened. She then explains that she has passed all of her topics, but many of them with the minimum passing grades, which has given her a low grade-point average.

"But, Mother, do you remember our agreement when I was in the eighth grade? You wanted to finish the twelfth grade. And now you have. Why not celebrate?"

Slapping her books with her hand as she speaks, Mother announces that she does not want to only finish twelfth grade, she wants to pass Tawjihi exams with a high grade-point average that qualifies her for a scholarship. She dreams of entering college, too, graduating and becoming a high school teacher.

Because West Bank college scholarships for literary students are granted mainly to those with the highest grade-point averages, leaving the majority of students to compete for them, Father assures Mother that he will do everything in his power to support her during the next year and until she becomes the teacher she dreams of becoming.

My parents now seem on good terms. Mother feels that she can have her dreams and her marriage, too. Father's fears about Mother's schooling have turned into pride in her strong spirit and persistence. My parents decide to move to a new house in al-Bireh, Ramallah's twin city. We will live in al-Sharafa district, on the edge of Jerusalem Street, and we'll have four bedrooms, a large living room with a telephone, a backyard and a front yard where my younger siblings can play freely, and a shed where father can have a goat. He has missed having one. It has been years since I heard him singing happily to his goat. I am eager for that to happen.

Father also stops driving permanently when Muhammad decides to get a job as a truck driver. Father will work cutting stones and building houses only. But knowing how fond Father is of trucks, Muhammad promises every now and then to let Father drive his truck.

Grandmother Fatima comes from Jerusalem to visit our new house. Her basket is filled with pomegranates because Mother loves them. When I embrace Grandma to welcome her I suddenly notice that I have grown taller than she is, and I tell her that.

"Maybe because of all the books that you are standing on," she jokes, and glances at my feet.

Grandma is wearing a newly embroidered traditional dress. The charcoal-black fabric is hand-stitched with red, green, orange, and pink threads creating the shapes of flowers, birds, and stars. She is also wearing her full traditional headdress. The scarf is jasmine-flower white, and under it she has her *saffah*, the cap adorned with pierced silver coins that are sewn on to create a crown. A wealthier Palestinian woman would have gold coins crowning her *saffah*. Grandma's round face glows like a harvest moon as she moves from room to room in our new house.

When done, she sits and I bring her a cup of tea. She begins to share news of other family members. But all Mother wants to talk about is how hard she has worked to get to this moment. Grandma nods her head over and over to let Mother know that she hears what Mother says.

Remembering that Grandma cannot read even a word, and therefore cannot relate to Mother's experience, I ask if she is willing to learn something so simple and yet so important that it changes a person's life forever.

"Yes," Grandma replies.

So I put a pencil in her hand, hold it against a piece of paper, and trace an image slowly. Mother watches across the table as though a magic show is happening.

Grandma has no idea what I am doing but lets me move her hand. For a moment, she tries to pull away but then decides to go with me. When we are done Grandma does not know what the shape on the paper is.

"*F*, the first letter of your name, Grandma Fatima," I say, "and you wrote it. The Tawjihi journey and then going to college begin with writing one letter and one word. I started when I was three and a half years old when I learned to write *alef*, the first letter of my name."

Grandma gazes at her pencil, smiles like a child, then looks at me and asks me to teach her another.

TO LEARN MORE

You are invited to explore the following resources, which shed more light on the issues related to Palestine and the Palestinians:

United Nations Relief and Works Agency for Palestine Refugees in the Near East websites: www.unrwa.org and http://archive.unrwa.org
These UN-run websites are rich with the history of the UNRWA, from its inception to the present time. They include statistics, images, videos, hopeful initiatives in refugee camps, a newsroom, and up-to-date information about the five million Palestinian refugees registered with the United Nations.

Institute for Middle East Understanding (www.imeu.org)
The IMEU is a US-based organization that provides readers with journalistic reports, historical facts, current news analysis, and a multitude of digital resources about Palestine and Palestinians.

East Jerusalem, / West Jerusalem (A film produced by Gidi Avivi, 2014).
This is a documentary film starring Israeli, Palestinian, Jewish, Christian, and Muslim musicians, including singer-songwriter David Broza and singer Mira Awad, who all embark

on a quest to set aside the harsh political reality, transcend for a short time the separation between Israelis and Palestinians, and record an album.

Being Palestinian: Personal Reflections on Palestinian Identity in the Diaspora, edited by Yasir Suleiman (Edinburgh: Edinburgh University Press, 2016).

Being Palestinian is an anthology of short essays that brings together one hundred two Palestinians living outside the Arab world, mainly in the United States and Europe. Each author reflects on the experience of the Palestinian identity in the diaspora.

Palestine: Peace Not Apartheid by Jimmy Carter (New York: Simon & Schuster, 2006) and **We Can Have Peace in the Holy Land: A Plan That Will Work** by Jimmy Carter (New York: Simon & Schuster, 2010).

These books provide a unique perspective of a former US president regarding Palestine and Israel and the search for peace. Relevant to the *Balcony on the Moon* timeline, Carter was the US president from 1977 to 1981. He won the Nobel Peace Prize in 2002.

The People Around You!

An optimal way a person learns about the world is by forming friendships across cultures. In your community or in your school, it is likely that there are Palestinians, Arabs, Muslims,

Christians, Jews, and many Middle Eastern people who can share their perspectives about what you read and enrich your journey, as well as let you enrich theirs.

Author's Website
(www.ibtisambarakat.com)

Visit the author's website for questions and answers about *Balcony on the Moon*, and to hear the author read a section from the book. You will find a lesson plan that includes learning to speak some Arabic expressions, as well as additional creative resources.

Shukran / Thank You:

Majed A. Wahhab
Rima Tarazi
Elise Crohn
Ann Mehr
Tracy L. Barnett
Kris Meilahn
Jane Franck
Joan McElroy
Munther Salah
Nabil Alawi
Suzanne Fisher Staples
Naomi Shihab Nye
John Schmeiding
Melanie Kroupa
Barbara Grzeslo
Victor Navasky
Neil Barsky
Steve Weinberg
Margaret Ferguson

Susan Dobinick and everyone at FSG/Macmillan
who helped to create this book,
readers of *Tasting the Sky* who encouraged me
to write more about being Palestinian,

reader Madeleine Fenn, who tattooed a line
from *Tasting the Sky* on her arm and sent me
a photograph so that I could
see the impact of the book on her,
and my friend, the moon.